Reversing Urban Decline

The Winthrop-Kenmore Corridor in the
Edgewater and Uptown Communities of Chicago

Ed Marciniak

National Center for Urban Ethnic Affairs

This report was prepared under a grant from the Ford Foundation. Portions of Chapter 1 have appeared in *Planning for the City's Social Environment*, a report prepared for the Department of Planning of the City of Chicago by Ed Marciniak in 1980.

©1981 Ed Marciniak

**Printed in the United States of America
All rights reserved
Library of Congress Catalog Card #81-80100
ISBN-0-940-798-00-X**

The cartoon on page 85 is reprinted with permission from *Modern Maturity*, published by the American Association of Retired Persons. The photograph on page 18 is by Arlys Dockendorff. The quotation on page 76 is from *The Other America* by Michael Harrington, © 1962, Macmillan Publishing Co.

Contents

Foreword by Msgr. Geno C. Baroni

Preface

1 Neighborhoods as Seedbeds of Revitalization 1

2 Uptown, Edgewater and Their Connecting Corridor 10

3 Edgewater Threatened 26

4 Thirteen Neighborhoods But a Single Community 50

5 Hard Choices: The Limits of Planning 65

6 Urban Strategies That Work 79

7 The Future of the Winthrop-Kenmore Corridor 104

Foreword

The failure of American urban policy in recent decades has been its unwillingness to see the city, if not the world itself, as an intercultural village held together by social networks. Today, those who fashion public policy have begun to recognize that viable neighborhoods are fundamental to the revitalization of cities. These neighborhoods reflect the presence of social, cultural, religious and economic institutions, those voluntary associations whose interaction forms a vital network. These, says Edmund Burke, are the "platoons of affection" where the values and loyalties of people are lodged.

In the nineteenth century Alexis de Tocqueville marveled at the ease with which Americans developed voluntary social groups. More recently, Jane Jacobs and E. F. Schumacher have stressed the importance of those voluntary social networks through which a community negotiates its interest with the public or private decision-makers who affect their lives. In that same tradition, Ed Marciniak scrutinizes neighborhoods. With understanding and sensitivity, he recognizes the importance of these networks, legitimates the role of community groups, and analyzes their resourcefulness in dealing with those forces of pluralism and diversity that can tear a city apart. He confirms René DuBos' view of the importance of these groups to building community by fostering the "tolerance for diversity that is necessary for survival."

In precise and insightful descriptions, *Reversing Urban Decline* examines a neighborhood from the inside, revealing its inner workings in a way rarely seen in the literature on urban policy. The book flies in the face of traditional planners who ignore the values, symbols and social networks of community. It was their failure to respect the human infrastructure of voluntary organizations and non-governmental groups that resulted in public housing projects like Pruitt-Igoe in St. Louis and Robert Taylor Homes in Chicago. To the peril of us all, these were pseudo-communities, planned and built without the people's involvement in their design.

Our strength as a nation comes from recognizing the intercultural imperative of our neighborhoods, the most diverse in the world. In re-emphasizing the values of voluntary, fraternal, and non-governmental associations, Marciniak's neighborhood study reminds us how essential they are to preserving the great promise of the American experiment which esteems "We the People" as the critical factor in the American covenant.

Msgr. Geno C. Baroni

Preface

Neighborhoods, says a critic, are like valentines, laced with sentiment, negligible in significance and easily misunderstood. My eyewitness account of several Chicago neighborhoods is unabashedly sentimental. But I hope it also illuminates their importance to the renascence of the city which claims them for its own.

The Chicago neighborhoods I chronicle and analyze are tenacious, resilient and inventive. They make up the north side community of Edgewater which fronts Lake Michigan and which was subjected to conflicting and debilitating pressures during the decades following World War II. Decisions downtown, in corporate headquarters and elsewhere, shaped the future of Edgewater and its sister community Uptown. Edgewater's many neighborhoods were vulnerable to the whim or wisdom of planners and geographers who worked in some remote hideaway, drawing their colorful maps without contributions or interference from local residents. In the 1970s these neighborhoods became energizers of urban change. Their leaders, their pragmatism, their political know-how and their optimism kindled, in the larger community to which they belonged, a determination to halt the forces of urban decline and to arrest the decay from within and from without.

A current school of social thought regards the urban neighborhood as dead or dying, a bit of old-fashioned nostalgia to delight the historical imagination and then to be dismissed. Whether or not this is true in other places, I contend that the dynamism which keeps Chicago vital is due in part to the human transactions, mutual support and humane interaction which neighborhoods nurture and protect. In the 1970s the residents of Chicago's Edgewater fashioned a future for their community through neighborhoods that were alive, stable and increasingly secure. In the 1980s the adjoining community of Uptown has the opportunity to revive and begin rebuilding its commercial and residential core after having failed, in earlier decades, to forestall an avalanche of deterioration. My study explains the reasons for Edgewater's renewed sense of confidence and for Uptown's second chance at revitalization. Edgewater's destiny, intertwined with Uptown's, is the primary concern of this study.

A special word of appreciation is owed the Ford Foundation which provided a grant which enabled me to complete this report.

E.M.

1

Neighborhoods as Seedbeds of Revitalization

Conventional wisdom says that cities used to work, that they once enhanced the good life for their residents, whether newcomers or oldtimers. The same folklore suggests that cities of the northern United States, such as Chicago, Cleveland, New York or Detroit, no longer perform well, no longer provide for the good life as they once did or at least appeared to do. At best, this may be a partial truth, arising out of a misunderstanding of what the conventional wisdom was seeking to explain.

The real wisdom, perhaps, is that the American city taken as a whole never really worked very efficiently, or functioned satisfactorily. Instead, the functioning urban units were the city's diverse neighborhoods. Because neighborhood life was vigorous, the city itself appeared to be thriving. Within the neighborhoods, social and religious institutions made urbanization more humane and tolerable, bolstering the family, supplying adolescents with an identity, often ethnic and/or religious, and giving the young and the elderly a point of reference, some place from which they came or to which they could return. A Chicagoan could say, "I live in Edgewater" or "I come from Bridgeport" or "I'm from Back of the Yards."

Back in the 1940s, urban neighborhoods came under attack. One by one they were swamped by racial transition or obliterated by expressways built to link the city's center with the sprawling suburban ring. They tumbled before bulldozers clearing the way for hospital parking lots, university halls, shopping centers and industrial parks. They were ignored by insensitive "downtown" planners or deserted by a generation who, in pursuit of different values, fled to the suburbs.

Now that many neighborhoods have disappeared and others continue to be threatened, cities are unmistakably in trouble. There is a connection: with their neighborhoods less visible or doing poorly, the woes of the cities themselves dramatically come to the fore. Most publicized are the failure of large cities to maintain financial stability and their weaknesses in urban governance. These pressing matters then preoccupy the agendas of investment bankers, political scientists, federal officials, governors, but most of all mayors, the chief executives of large cities. But in doing so, they ignore the historic role of the urban neighborhood.

For urban newcomers, from one generation to the next, the city itself symbolized human accomplishment, where dreams — personal, ethnic, or religious — could be fulfilled. But it was in the city's neighborhoods that the immigrant achievements were realized — not in City Hall or a downtown office. Since newcomers were the lifeblood of cities, healthy neighborhoods contributed far more to the overall well-being of cities than scholars or planners had previously been willing to acknowledge. This fresh understanding explains, in great part, the renewed interest in the future of urban neighborhoods and in their importance to urban revitalization.

Many great cities of the western world rebuilt their vital centers every century or two, usually through the initiative of the national government, as in Paris under Napoleon III and his chief planner Haussmann; through urban renewal following a disastrous war as in Berlin; through a catastrophic fire or earthquake as in London in 1669, Chicago in 1871 or San Francisco in 1906. In the United States, however, large-scale rebuilding of urban centers has been postponed with dire results. As the American society began to recover from World War I, some urban reconstruction took place in the 1920s. However, in every decade since, a concerted and sustained push to revitalize the older urban cores of large U.S. cities has been undertaken only piecemeal or put off because of:

— the onset of the Great Depression in the 1930s;

— U.S. involvement in World War II during the 1940s;

— federal priorities to expand the nation's suburbs in the 1950s in order to house new family formations which had been deferred by the war;

— the nation's preoccupation in the 1960s with violent confrontations on city streets, the national movement to guarantee the civil rights of blacks and the national diversion of resources to meet the heavy U.S. commitment in Southeast Asia.

Finally in the 1970s the United States took a searching look at its urban areas and started to do slowly what had been left undone for decades: finish the rebuilding of the inner core of the nation's older cities.

Reassessing Urban Policy

Faced with this challenge, urban planners at every governmental level went through agonizing reappraisals of their assumptions and strategies about the best way to rebuild U. S. cities. The American Society of Planning Officials devoted its annual planning conference in 1971 to an urban theme: "The Making of National Growth Policy." After a year-long study, the American Institute of Architects published in 1972 its major proposal for urban planning, entitled *Strategy for Building a Better America.*

There were still other reasons for the reassessment of traditional ways to rebuild and revitalize cities. During the 1950s, 1960s and early 1970s, years of deepening decline and growing unrest in large, older cities, the federal government spent more than $100 billion to bail out cities through programs such as urban renewal, public housing, slum clearance, FHA and other housing subsidies, employment training, juvenile delinquency prevention, crime deterrence, aid to dependent children, the war against poverty, Model Cities and financial help to inner city schools. It is now generally believed that this federal presence did indeed help alleviate many stubborn urban problems, but others worsened and new ones came to light.

The shortcomings of federally-funded programs to fight poverty, rid cities of slums, end racial discrimination and segregation, upgrade education, decrease unemployment or cut crime were acknowledged by the mid-1970s. The *Public Interest* quarterly, for example, devoted several issues to an assessment of federal programs targeted for cities. Its special issue in the winter of 1974 was entitled: "The Great Society: Lessons for the Future." By the middle 1970s it was not surprising to find the federal government shifting the planning and programming responsibility for urban revitalization back to cities through large block grants.

Establishing the Importance of Neighborhoods

In Washington, as well as back in the local municipalities, urban planners began taking a second look at the pivotal importance of livable, safe neighborhoods and communities to the future of cities and to the good life of their inhabitants.

One of the first signals that the highly centralized, federally dominated approach to urban revitalization was losing support came from the American Institute of Architects. In its *Strategy for Building a Better America*, the AIA proposed in 1972 that "the neighborhood should be America's growth unit," asserting that:

> Americans, whoever they are and however many there may be. . . are searching for communities that are more livable. . .neighborhoods that are safe, neighborhoods that are within easier reach of jobs and a richer mix of community life and services, neighborhoods small enough to have some identity of their own, where no one need be anonymous while attaining the privacy Americans always have yearned for.
>
> It follows, we think, that the measuring rod of national growth should be the quality of the neighborhoods, and the assurance that neighborhoods — even when they change — will not deteriorate. The neighborhood should be America's growth unit.

Later, the AIA reaffirmed its basic policy for planning cities, saying that the nation's:

> long term policy goal. . .must encourage the restoration of the neighborhood as the cornerstone of community life, both in the scale of its design and in its social function.

There were other signs of a changing attitude toward the reconstruction of cities. Early in 1977, Leon S. Eplan, president of the American Institute of Planners and the Commissioner of Budget and Planning for Atlanta, reinforced the view articulated earlier by the AIA:

> We no longer believe, as we did in the 1960s, that governments can rebuild cities. We believe that people are the only city builders. The role of government today is far more limited. . . . What we lost during this period of change was not simply housing and neighborhoods, but the bonds that tie people together: the garden clubs, boy scouts, PTAs, civic clubs and church groups. This is the social fabric around which people build their collective lives and evolve themselves, through which they share responsibility for their fellow man.

In a survey of city planning agencies in 1978, *Personality, Politics and Planning: How City Planners Work*, authors Anthony James Catanese and W. Paul Farmer concluded that:

> Perhaps the most striking [innovation] is the sincere and major commitment and accompanying set of practices and programs for the preservation, restoration and improvement of neighborhoods in the city. . . . The reason we use the word striking to describe this innovation is because it is not widely heralded in the literature of planning (although some of the popular press has featured such programs). . . we consider this movement to a neighborhood level of planning the most significant of city planning practices described as innovations by the city planners we talked with. . . .

Four national developments corroborated the finding of Catanese and Farmer about the growing concern of urban planners for the future of neighborhoods:

● The National Commission on Neighborhoods was created by Congress in 1978, its members appointed by President Jimmy Carter. The new Commission was prompted by the widespread realization that federal programs and urban planning in the 1960s and 1970s had largely neglected, and had even victimized, the urban neighborhoods of this nation. Thus the Commission saw its main purpose as redressing this imbalance and developing a planning strategy that would "help neighborhoods help themselves." The Commission report, *People, Building Neighborhoods: The Final Report to the President and the Congress of the United States*, was published in 1979.

● For the first time in history, the U.S. Bureau of the Census agreed to supply local municipalities with a "substantial set of statistics" taken from the 1980 Census of Population and Housing for each neighborhood which local officials recognize to be part of "their neighborhood systems." This new service of the Bureau of the Census responded to the reappearance of the neighborhood as a major priority of local governmental officials as they looked ahead to planning activities during the 1980s.

● In 1977 the President of the United States authorized the formation of an Office of Neighborhoods, Voluntary Associations and Consumer Protection within the U.S. Department of Housing and Urban Development. It provided HUD with a staff whose major responsibility was to act as an advocate of neighborhoods and to relate this concern to the work of municipal planning departments. Officially speaking, neighborhoods were no longer to be treated as federal colonies, subject to periodic invasions by city and federal programs over which residents had little or no control. To head this office the President appointed a man who had emerged in the 1970s as a national champion of neighborhoods, Monsignor Geno C. Baroni, then president of the National Center for Urban Ethnic Affairs in Washington, D.C.

● Finally, in the 1970s large cities like Chicago, Atlanta, Seattle and others elected new mayors who successfully campaigned on a pledge to make the top priority of their new administration the improvement, stabilization and development of city neighborhoods. In cities across the continent, the renewed emphasis on neighborhoods dramatically revived the social dimension of urban planning — by conserving existing neighborhoods or finding new ways to promote community sub-areas of the city.

Changing Municipal Strategies

By the early 1970s it had become apparent, to municipal officials everywhere in the U.S., that traditional land-use planning and the federal programming of the 1960s had too often proved impotent or inadequate in achieving the revitalization of aging areas in the inner city. New approaches to unsolved urban problems were being sought. The rising cost of new housing in the suburbs, for example, made the existing stock of housing in many older city neighborhoods more attractive.

Planners and public officials were awakened to understand that major policy decisions affecting urban areas were clearly not questions solely of physical urban redevelopment. Issues like the high concentration of single-parent families in public housing developments; the need to devise new ways to move populations dependent on public aid into the world of constructive work; high infant mortality; high truancy and drop-out rates in inner city high schools; and the abiding concern for safe sidewalks all obviously demanded a response beyond the ken of conventional city planners.

City officials no longer remained passive before federal and state policies which previously had had a disastrous impact upon some neighborhoods, such as the "deinstitutionalization" of a state hospital's mental patients with the resultant inundation of receiving neighborhoods; the destructive impact of public aid payments upon the existing supply of rental housing; public housing projects which resulted in dehumanizing concentrations of the new underclass (single-parent households, multi-problem families, unemployable adults, drug addicts, and alcoholics); or the ruinous consequences of the Federal Housing Administration's lending practices upon stable home ownership and neighborhood vitality. Such federal and state policies were coming under intensive scrutiny and criticism locally. Increasingly, municipal officials were seeking to determine in advance the neighborhood impact of the thrust and implementation of new federal and state initiatives.

The willingness of many city officials to deal with the neighborhood agenda could also be traced directly to the increasing ability of community groups to participate in the urban planning process. Although they continued to speak out and assert their independence, many were now ready to do this in a posture of partnership. The community-based groups insisted that they had a contribution to make to community planning and that all of the answers were not to be found in city halls. Municipal leadership came to recognize that the support and participation of the local community and its institutions could help ensure the success of City programs and projects. A vital public-private partnership could preserve and rehabilitate housing and neighborhoods alike.

Self-conscious neighborhoods are among the more powerful energizers of urban revitalization. They stimulate the larger urban

Edgewater and Uptown Communities in City of Chicago

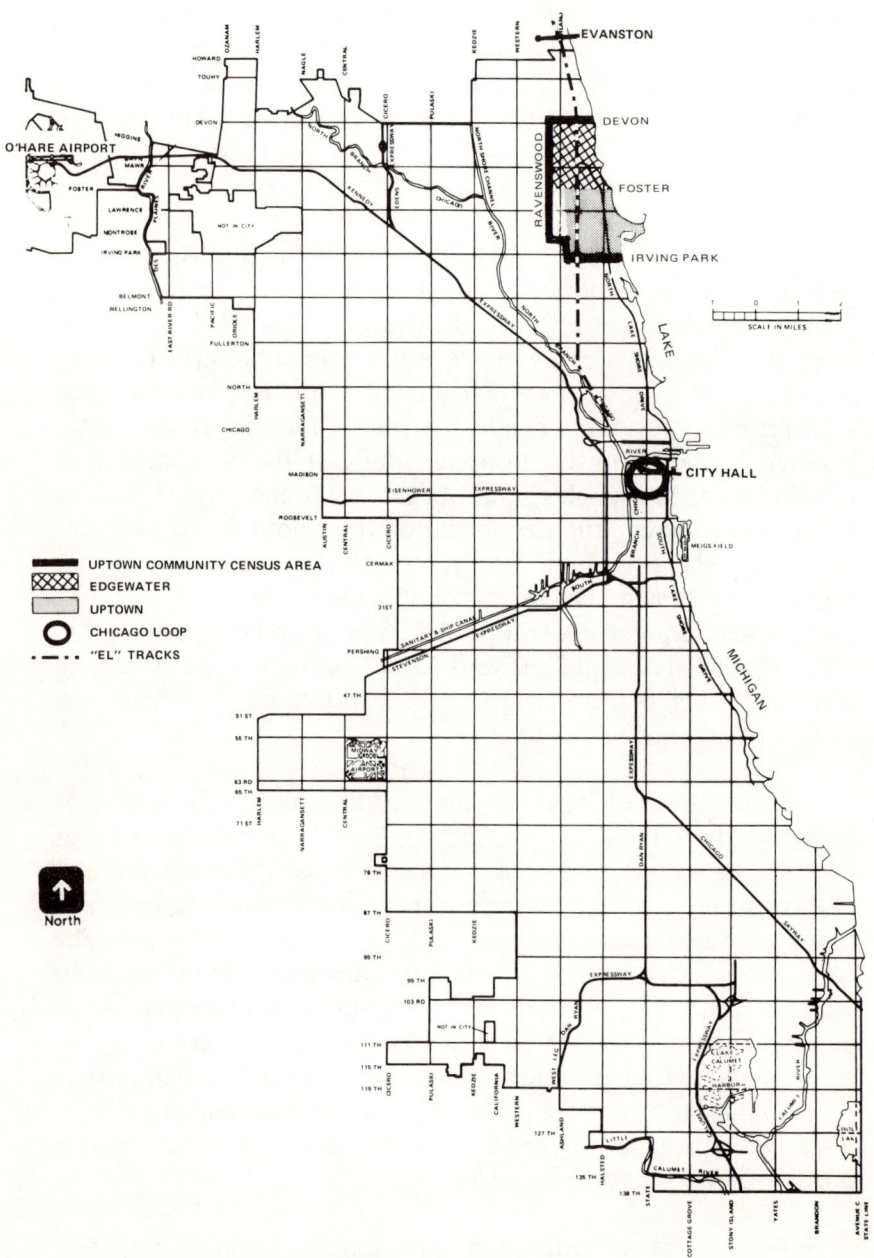

community; their influence penetrates city hall and reaches the civic and business establishment headquartered downtown. On the other hand, they function as conservators, resisting rapid change so that they can cope with it. When neighborhoods reassert themselves, they inevitably shape the destiny of the larger community of which they are a part. The pages that follow describe how the Edgewater community worked to arrest decline; how its neighborhoods organized themselves and sparked urban change. But Edgewater is joined to the Uptown community, like a Siamese twin, by a connecting corridor of north and south streets and a public transit line. Thus the condition of Uptown's health affects Edgewater's vitality—and vice versa.

2

Uptown, Edgewater and Their Connecting Corridor

Today the Uptown community, once a showplace, persists in evoking memories of earlier glories. It had been a residential mecca for the middle class as far back as the early 1900s, with elegant mansions for older wealthy families and spacious apartments for professionals and junior executives. It was Chicago's *bon ton* in the 1920s, a touch of class in an era of ragtime and Art Deco. The high spot of its golden age was the baroque splendor of the Aragon Ballroom and two velvet and gilt movie palaces, Balaban & Katz' Riviera and Uptown theaters on Broadway Avenue. Balaban & Katz then added two more theaters, Pantheon and Lakeside on Sheridan Road, spotlighting again Uptown's pre-eminence as a motion picture center.

Uptown is agreeably situated on Lake Michigan, six miles north of Chicago's downtown "Loop" business district. In the 1880s and 1890s excellent mass transit brought Uptown its residents; in later decades it was prosperity and public attention that attracted them. An elevated commuter railroad passed through Uptown on its way to suburban Evanston, three miles farther north. Electrically powered street cars connected with the elevated train line, linking two parallel east and west commercial streets, Wilson and Lawrence Avenues. Additional north and south transportation was provided along Sheridan Road and Broadway Avenue, creating a transportation hub four blocks in diameter. In the era before automobiles engulfed the city, mass transportation greatly accelerated Uptown's growth.

By the middle 1920s, Uptown had become one of Chicago's most successful business centers. It boasted two large banks, a handsome office building for doctors, lawyers and dentists, elegant restaurants and two movie theaters which attracted well-dressed crowds day and night. With 4,400 seats for cinema fans, the Uptown theater was the largest movie house in the city. Prior to World War I, Uptown even became one of the nation's better known centers for the production of silent films. Essanay studios, producing the early films of Charles Chaplin and Gloria Swanson, built its headquarters here, as did smaller movie producers. To add to the splendor, many film stars took up residence in the area.

According to Patrick McCormick, a resident of Uptown before World War II:

> The exuberant and optimistic investors in the district even tried to induce the "Broadway Limited," the well-traveled train running between Chicago and New York City, to establish its terminal at the building on the northwest corner of Broadway and Wilson Avenue.

Around this dazzling commercial center, hundreds of three-story apartment buildings sprang up to meet the growing demand for rental housing. Elevator apartment hotels of nine stories and more added to the high density. Uptown became one of the most heavily populated areas in the United States. Before the economic earthquake of the Great Depression struck in the 1930s, vacant land in Uptown was almost impossible to find.

Uptown had profited as much from the enterprise of businessmen as from its access to good transportation. When merchants in the area around Wilson and Broadway Avenues sought to unify and publicize their venture in the early 1920s, they hit upon the name Uptown, borrowing it from a fashionable department store so named, for their bustling shopping district. As its popularity increased, the name was extended to the surrounding residential area, to the setting as well as to the jewel.

Edgewater: the Neighboring Community to the North

A sister community of the bejeweled Uptown was the Edgewater community, the name given to a subdivision within a larger suburban tract which was annexed by Chicago in 1889. (See illustration on page 13.)

Even after annexation, Edgewater continued to be regarded as a suburb. A visitors' guide to the Chicago World's Columbian Exposition in 1893 called Edgewater "one of the prettiest suburbs in the country." Along the community's eastern edge on the lakefront, the Edgewater Beach Hotel opened its doors in 1916, becoming a luxury resort with a national reputation. Its acres of landscaped and flowering terraces, "The Boardwalk" for dining and dancing under the stars, and its 1,000 rooms made the Edgewater hotel a landmark. A radio station in the hotel beamed dance music from the Marine Dining Room to listeners of the jazz era; the nation's top entertainers burnished their reputations here. The elevated line rumbling two blocks to the west called public attention to this residential development in the early 1900s by naming the nearest stations Edgewater and North Edgewater.

Edgewater's development, in contrast to Uptown's, was predominantly residential. Edgewater's portion of Broadway Avenue offered small convenient stores for brief shopping trips, while the residents made frequent use of Uptown's large and prosperous business district when planning more extensive purchases. Edgewater and Uptown shared one striking feature: the elevated commuter line, popularly known as the "El," which became the catalyst for intensive residential use of every foot of available land. East of the railroad tracks, Edgewater's housing construction resembled Uptown's: elevator apartment hotels with furnished rooms; walk-up residential buildings containing as many as sixty-four apartments or as few as six; and a little farther away, close to the lake, gracious single-family homes or three-story buildings with luxurious apartments. The most crowded residential development took place wherever the elevated train stopped, every two or three blocks, to unload or pick up passengers.

West of Broadway Avenue and the elevated line the new housing being built was Chicago Traditional: single and two-family detached homes varying in elegance, family homes for less well-to-do families with children; occasional three-story apartments; and six-flat buildings squaring off the corner lots.

THE MAKING OF EDGEWATER

The following advertisement for Edgewater appeared in the June 19, 1887 issue of the Chicago *Tribune* and represents one of the first newspaper advertisements for the new suburb. The original was in a single one-inch column.

EDGEWATER

Where Is It?

Situated Three Miles North of Lincoln Park on the Evanston Division of C.M. & St. Paul R.R. Shore of Lake Michigan.

EDGEWATER

What Is It?

It is the only Electric Lighted Suburb Adjacent to Chicago.

It is reached in 23 minutes by rail from Union Depot. Frequent Trains and Low Fare.

EDGEWATER

What Has It?

IT HAS Elegant Houses of Different modern and artistic designs. Queen Anne and Colonial Styles prevailing, well built, having all the latest improvements in plumbing.

IT HAS Macadamized Streets, Stone Sidewalks, and Stone Curbing. Every Street lighted with Electric Lights.

IT HAS many natural advantages being on the lake shore, undulating and dry ground, and is well wooded.

IT HAS Electric Lights (Edison incandescent in every house and in every room, which costs much less than gas).

IT HAS water in every house, supplied from Lake View Water Works—a plentiful supply of pure water always.

EDGEWATER

IT HAS the Lake Front and Beach, affording admirable facilities for boating and bathing. The beach is sandy and slopes gradually.

IT HAS a beautiful view of Lake Michigan. Nearly all the shipping from and to Chicago can be seen from Edgewater.

IT HAS a perfect system of Underground Drainage.

IT HAS Two Stores and a Hall, a telegraph and Express Office, and Public Telephone.

IT HAS MORE ADVANTAGES THAN ANY SUBURB OF CHICAGO. It is within convenient driving distance of the city. Beautiful houses, splendid views, plenty of shade, telegraph, telephone, express office, stores, perfect drainage, and moderate prices.

Besides convenient shopping and efficient rapid transit, what were the magnets that drew Chicago's rising middle class to Edgewater and Uptown in the decades immediately before and after World War I? The first was the social status associated with a highly urban community containing the most modern (for those days) apartments. Uptown and Edgewater offered an idealized social setting, a fashionable world inside the city limits for a new generation scrambling up the social and economic ladder.

Then there was Lake Michigan, with its changing vistas, its shoreline parks and its sandy beaches. The Lake was only a few blocks east of the elevated right-of-way. It was nature's—and God's—gift to the homegrown middle class as they shopped for housing away from Chicago's center but not as far as the suburbs. Riding the rapid transit or, in later years, driving up the tree-lined lakefront boulevards, the new urban class could escape the city's commercial core, avoiding its pollution and congestion, while skipping the immigrant poverty and sub-standard housing in-between, on their way to Uptown or Edgewater. The lakefront boulevard was described in 1900 as "one of the handsomest carriage ways in the world."

Attractive Communities

The historical and physical resemblances between Uptown and Edgewater were real, but in special ways. The two neighboring communities, both bordering the lake, could together be divided into three strips running north and south—each nearly three miles long. The eastern section was oriented to the lake and its visual and natural amenities, such as the swath of beaches and lakeside parks. The western portion of Edgewater and Uptown was populated with one vital neighborhood after another. The neighborhoods of Uptown were more fragmented and less contiguous because of the presence of two historic landmarks, St. Bonifacius and Graceland cemeteries, the latter providing the last resting place for many of Chicago's founding fathers. The strength of Edgewater's neighborhoods came from its institutions, such as the Protestant and Catholic churches which were rich in local history, inheriting the ethnic traditions of German, Irish and Scandinavian settlers.

The Connecting Corridor

Down the middle of Edgewater and Uptown ran a third strip, called the Winthrop-Kenmore corridor, wedged between the eastern lakefront section and the vigorous neighborhoods to the west. The corridor was, and still is, a unique urban configuration. Its spine was the elevated transit line running north and south parallel to Lake Michigan. In width, the corridor was less than two city blocks. Its western boundary was Broadway Avenue, a wide commercial street with department stores, taverns, warehouses, banks, auto sales rooms, restaurants, real estate offices, retail supermarkets, garages and convenience stores. The corridor's eastern edge ran up to Sheridan Road, the local thoroughfare nearest the lake and its parkland, one of the city's oldest and most elegant boulevards. (See map on page 16.)

The corridor borrowed its name from the two residential streets, Winthrop and Kenmore, which ran down its middle just east of the elevated line. After 1900, the housing bordering these streets was built with the highest densities possible, to take advantage of the rapid transit line's access to business and industrial districts at the city center. Along these streets were constructed high-rise buildings with spacious apartments numbering eight or nine rooms and three baths; twelve-story hotels with small kitchenette apartments; single-family residences; and a respectable number of comfortable, three-story, walk-up apartment buildings (See photograph on page 18.) Train stations, spaced every two or three blocks, served the corridor at nine places and flooded each east-west street with enough pedestrians to support small shops, variety stores, delicatessens and taverns.

The residential corridor begins in the heart of Uptown, in the business center, and runs north for approximately eighteen city blocks, two-thirds of them in Edgewater. It ends abruptly at Devon Avenue, at the entrance to the main campus of Loyola University. Founded by the Jesuits in the nineteenth century on Chicago's near west side, the University was relocated on the north side in 1909. Near by, but built later, are Mundelein College for women and the Academy of the Sacred Heart, a private elementary and secondary school. All three are Catholic educational institutions, Loyola University by far the largest and most influential. As the world of

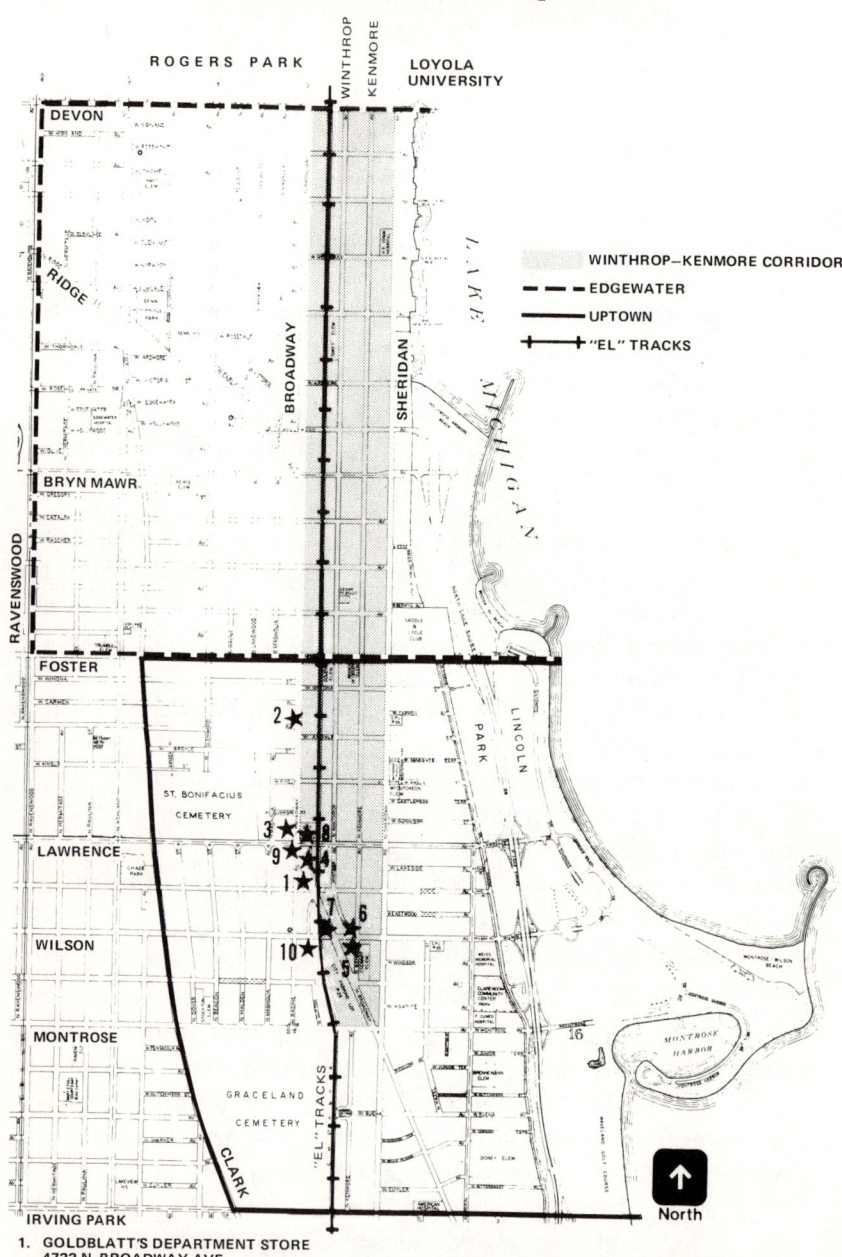

The Winthrop-Kenmore Corridor in Edgewater and Uptown

1. GOLDBLATT'S DEPARTMENT STORE
   4722 N. BROADWAY AVE.
2. COMBINED INSURANCE COMPANY OF AMERICA
   5050 N. BROADWAY AVE.
3. UPTOWN THEATER
   4816 N. BROADWAY AVE.
4. UPTOWN NATIONAL BANK
   4753 N. BROADWAY AVE.
5. UPTOWN FEDERAL SAVINGS AND LOAN
   4545 N. BROADWAY AVE.
6. BANK OF CHICAGO
   1050 W. WILSON AVE.
7. WILSON AVENUE "EL" STATION
8. LAWRENCE AVENUE "EL" STATION
9. RIVIERA THEATER
   4746 N. RACINE AVE.
10. TRUMAN COLLEGE
    1145 W. WILSON AVE.

commerce characterized the corridor's southern end, educational institutions dominated its northern tip.

The Winds of Change

The stability of the corridor was threatened in the middle 1920s. In 1925, the Chicago metropolitan area had 500,000 automobile owners, and Uptown began to feel their impact. Uptown's commercial character had been designed to accommodate pedestrians and mass transit users. Its retail center could no longer cope with the escalating demand for parking space. To add to Uptown's difficulties, the City in 1933 completed the extension of Lake Shore Drive north to Foster Avenue. Auto and bus traffic could now by-pass the business center in Uptown. Well-to-do residents who owned motor vehicles enjoyed a speedy and scenic route that avoided the congestion of the business district. The new drive was built not on existing lakefront land but on more than two square miles of land-fill which extended the lakeside green belt several blocks into Lake Michigan. Thus Chicago's popular beaches and parks were relocated several blocks further east, putting their users farther away from the stores, theaters, saloons and transportation located in Uptown.

The spectacular growth of suburban Evanston further challenged Uptown's pre-eminence as a shopping center. As a suburb that grew up around the campus of Northwestern University, which was founded in 1851, Evanston attracted many of Chicago's wealthy merchants who, leaving Chicago's charred landscape after the Great Fire of 1871, erected grand residences there. According to one historian, these storekeepers displayed "an enlightened taste and ready purse—two excellent things." Chicago's downtown department stores soon established branches in Evanston and competed vigorously for Uptown's retail customers. In his two-volume study, *Uptown: A Planning Report* published in 1962, urban planner Jack Meltzer singled out the suburb's advantage:

> Evanston's deleterious impact [upon Uptown] was due in part to the proximity of both of these centers to the same north-south transportation facilities.

Given a choice between shopping in Evanston or Uptown, many

18 *Reversing Urban Decline*

The Winthrop-Kenmore Corridor—1980

residents of Edgewater and its neighboring community to the north, Rogers Park, began using that mass transit line to buy clothing and household goods from more modern and fashionable stores in a suburban setting.

The final blow to Uptown's shaky economy came with the Great Depression of the 1930s. It was a financial shock from which Uptown never recovered. New housing construction stopped. Purchasing power declined among consumers generally, and the unemployed in particular. The retail business of local merchants was devastated; as independent stores in Uptown and elsewhere folded one by one, they were replaced by absentee-owned chain stores.

While Uptown's business district slumped in the 1930s, the surrounding residential blocks did not begin to deteriorate until a decade later, during World War II. Wartime changes brought their own kind of destruction to the housing which ringed Uptown's commercial center. Here, by the 1950s, was the city's second most densely populated square mile. Here was the southern — and vulnerable — end of the Winthrop-Kenmore corridor.

Workers who had poured into Chicago from all over the country in the 1940s in search of jobs in defense factories paid rent to landlords who readily cut up their apartment buildings into smaller furnished units. Most of the remodeling was hasty, shoddy, and cheap. The conversions were usually illegal, violated the City's building codes, but were tolerated by officials because of the severe housing shortage and national emergency. In an era of gas rationing and wartime cutbacks in auto production, Uptown's convenient transportation made small apartments a rental bargain.

The housing shortage eased in the 1950s. Suburban out-migration of Chicagoans began to expand dramatically. Newlyweds, with

---

On the opposite page, the panoramic view (looking southwest) of Winthrop and Kenmore Avenues reveals the mix of housing styles in four blocks of the corridor—two in Uptown (above) and two in Edgewater (below). The new high-rise (center left) is a private development, built with federal subsidy, for senior citizens. Just below it is the historic Epworth Methodist Church. At the extreme lower left can be seen a short slice of Sheridan Road.

babies on the way, found Uptown's tiny kitchenettes and small bedroom apartments far less appealing than the new ranch houses on suburban prairies. Furthermore, the house in the suburbs in the postwar decade could be bought cheaply, with a low down payment. The exodus included thousands of Edgewater and Uptown residents who, decades earlier, had striven mightily to move into these self-same communities. "Furnished Apartment" signs appeared on front doors, while on an upper floor, the inevitable dirty curtain hung out an open window and ruffled in the breeze.

Owners of Uptown's once-fashionable apartment hotels and three or four-story walk-ups found themselves with more vacancies than they could afford. They began to defer routine maintenance. Renting standards were lowered. The residential trends for the next three decades were set in motion. Early in the 1950s Uptown's vacancy rate rose to thirteen percent, twice the city-wide average, its vacancies beckoning a new kind of migrant. It had become a port of entry for American Indians from reservations out west and for whites from southern Appalachia, this trickle of migrants in the late 1940s turning into a steady stream by 1960. Both groups came from impoverished, rural backgrounds and possessed few job skills. For them, Uptown's obsolete apartments were urban havens. Overcrowding and misuse by careless tenants, coupled with little or no upkeep by the owners, accelerated the depreciation and deterioration of multi-family buildings. By 1960, according to Meltzer, Uptown contained approximately twenty-two percent of Chicago's supply of "deficient housing units," while housing only two percent of the city's total population.

Uptown's commercial artery, Broadway Avenue, was soon splotched with vacant stores and fly-by-night shopkeepers. When television invaded the nation, theater owners saw their patrons disappear, and delayed upkeep on their property which was no longer seen as a financial asset. Uptown's many theaters were no exception to the national trend. In many respects, Uptown's commercial decline was not unique; most of Chicago's neighborhood commercial strips were also in trouble. One Uptown proprietor stressed the phenomenon:

> Our tale of woe is like everybody else's. We are victims of the guerilla warfare between us and the large shopping centers under a

single management. We have a shortage of parking spaces, on and off the street; they have plenty. Nowadays, everybody has a car to transport themselves out of the neighborhood to a shopping place somewhere else.

In city neighborhoods like ours, ethnic and racial changes in population alter shopping patterns and buying habits. If you can't keep up with them, you may go bankrupt. What about the fact that the families with purchasing power have been moving to the suburbs while families with smaller pay checks and less spending money have been moving into our community?

In 1955, business and community leaders organized the Uptown Chicago Commission "as a forum for communication and as a catalyst for action." Five years later Uptown's business leaders were sufficiently aroused about the blight infecting the community to look for ways to halt decay and to stimulate public and private action that would lead to neighborhood revitalization. Under the aegis of the commission, Jack Meltzer undertook his two-volume study of Uptown. He summarized Uptown's conditions as follows:

Despite its many attributes, Uptown is in a state of decline. An estimated 40 to 50 percent of all existing housing units are the result of conversions; 52 percent of all housing units consist of one- and two-room units; and 27 percent lack adequate plumbing facilities. Approximately 300,000 square feet of ground floor retail space are either vacant or in marginal uses. About one-fifth (260) of the stores in the community are taverns, some of them with notorious reputation.... Increase in density during the past two decades has taken place through conversions rather than new construction. The speculative growth of Uptown's past periods of vitality has left its scars — the "dickie fronts," the rows of vacant stores — along the major arteries of the community. Misused public open space, inadequate facilities for vehicular movement and parking, these only begin to catalogue Uptown's current physical inadequacies....

More than 600 residential buildings, out of a total of 2,800 in the community, are registered as rooming houses with the Board of Election Commissioners. The impact of conversions on the transformation of Uptown from a family to a "transient" area is obvious from the fact that 75 percent of the rooming houses are in converted houses and family apartments. Rooming houses in the classical sense of a regulated well-maintained boarding house are no longer in operation save in a few rare instances.

Uptown as the Inner City

By 1960, the heart of Uptown had finally become part of the "inner city," that urban place being abandoned by the private sector, whether businesses or not-for-profit institutions. In the inner city, churches and social institutions are weak, understaffed and underattended, struggling to pay fuel bills. First-class stores move elsewhere; marginal businessmen appear; retail stores are poorly maintained; and window displays, if there are any, are unattractive and dingy. Broken whiskey bottles and empty beer cans litter the streets. Doctors, dentists and lawyers are hard to find. Private investment in new or remodeled buildings is scarce. Newlyweds sacrifice to move to another neighborhood. The inner city is in trouble because the private sector is on the run. Private resources are anemic, local leadership is fearful, and owners are looking for the chance to escape.

From any point of view, the economic condition of a low income, inner city community, such as the center of Uptown, is a depressing situation. As stores and offices move or go out of business, few new businesses open up. Vacant stores multiply. "Redlining" becomes common. Fire and liability insurance at reasonable rates is extremely difficult to get — if available at all. The flow of credit into the community — for businessman and customer alike — continues to dry up. Street crime rises. Extortion by gangs, "protection money," becomes a medium of exchange. The fear of crime escalates and discourages resident use of streets in the evening. Overnight, home delivery of newspapers and milk disappears. Suddenly and ominously, folding iron gates show up in storefront windows. As an inner city community, Uptown became a city under siege.

Despite the energy and efforts of the Uptown Chicago Commission and others, Uptown had become too vulnerable — particularly its commercial center and the housing located in the corridor. By the 1960s and throughout the 1970s, Uptown had established itself as a revolving door community. It could no longer conceal its high transiency and its skid row, a street of taverns, flophouses and twenty-six agencies for day labor. In 1960, for example, sixty-one percent of the rooming house occupants had lived at their present address less than a year. (See map on page 24.) During 1965, at Stockton public school, nearly fifty percent of the students had been enrolled at another school during the previous year. Uptown's established reputation as a port of entry for American Indians and Appalachian whites was reinforced later by incoming waves of Cubans and other Hispanics, East Asians, Koreans, and Arabs.

When these migrations began to subside in the late 1960s, the State of Illinois, seeking to save money, instituted a policy that moved tens of thousands of its mental patients from state-operated asylums into communities like Uptown. In less than a decade the State, without really alerting City officials, had successfully shifted much of its financial and custodial responsibility for mental patients to Chicago's residential communities. By the early 1970s the state government had transformed several city neighborhoods into mental wards; most notable among them was Uptown with its vacant apartment hotels. The City's police officers functioned as orderlies. Firefighters became the emergency nurses who were summoned, often too late, to attend to self-inflicted wounds of anguished mental patients, to cases of arson, suicide, disastrous personal trauma and other human tragedies. State supervision was conspicuously absent. The care of these former wards of the state was mercilessly substandard. According to a spokesman for the Chicago Region of the Illinois Department of Mental Health, some 7,000 "deinstitutionalized" patients were shipped to Uptown in one year alone.

The 1960s were an era of federal bonanzas for urban areas. As federal monies began to flow freely, the City of Chicago opened one human service agency after another. Whenever an Uptown store or office shut its doors, a public or private welfare agency moved in. At least the new occupants could afford to pay the rent. An employment counsellor described the change:

> Uptown's center of gravity shifted to welfare. That became the main business and the biggest new source of jobs. With the help of the state, the Winthrop-Kenmore corridor was converted into the city's unofficial poorhouse on the north side.
>
> People used to live and work in Uptown. But now we're overrun by absentee landlords, precinct captains, policemen, teachers and social workers—all carpetbaggers.

Day Labor Agencies and Boarding Houses in the Winthrop-Kenmore Corridor

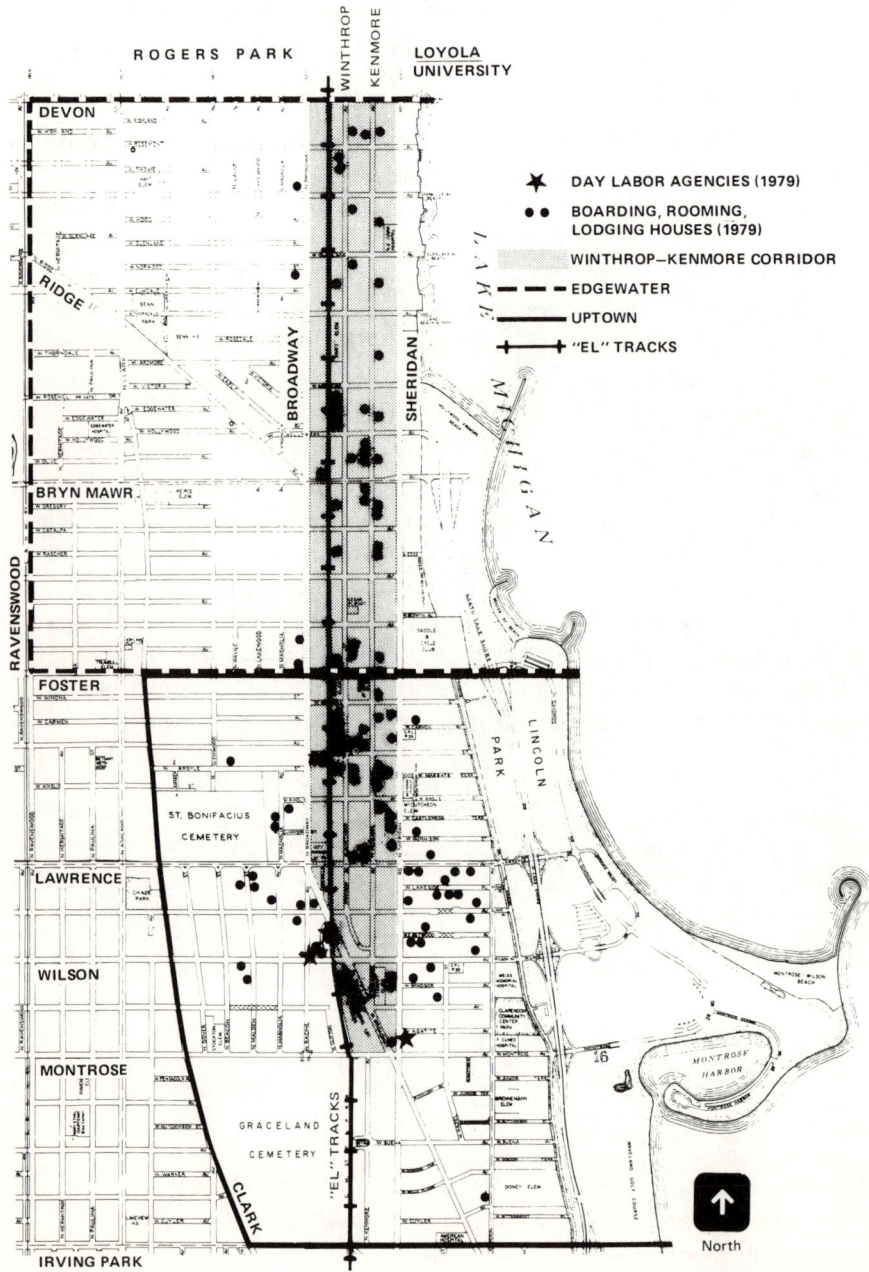

The multiplication of social welfare agencies and institutions confronts a residential community with a disturbing dilemma. An agency can indeed serve local residents in need of help, for example, alcoholics, heroin addicts, social deviates, mental patients, single-parent families, emotionally disturbed adults, juvenile delinquents, runaways, and others. If only two or three agencies open their doors, the community can usually cope with the population being served. But when the number of social agencies expands from three to thirty-three, the community's resilience to change is grievously weakened. The social fabric starts to tatter.

Crushed by transiency and lack of upkeep, Uptown's housing supply could no longer withstand the abuse. Most vulnerable were the three-story, multi-family apartment buildings, many of which had been cut up into smaller, furnished units. Not originally constructed for so many families with small children, the buildings deteriorated under the weight of overcrowding and heavy use. Whether owner-occupied or not, they experienced poor and deferred maintenance. Between 1960 and 1981, more than 4,000 housing units were demolished, leaving the Uptown section of the corridor looking as if it had been blitzed.

While the deterioration originally was concentrated at Uptown's commercial center and the lower end of the Winthrop-Kenmore corridor, the housing decay inevitably spread in all directions. It was resisted, with moderate success, in the western neighborhoods of the Uptown community. The blight also moved east, infecting the middle class residential areas closer to the lake. But principally the deterioration, together with the transient population, crept relentlessly northward along the corridor. As apartment buildings were demolished, transient renters and roomers packed up and moved north along Winthrop and Kenmore Avenues into similar buildings which in turn suffered the same fate.

In the late 1960s, Uptown's highly vulnerable populations, travelling up the defenseless corridor, began to move into Edgewater.

3

Edgewater Threatened

In the early 1930s, a distinguished team of University of Chicago sociologists in Hyde Park, fourteen miles south of Edgewater, divided Chicago into 75 community areas and began compiling census information by these areas. Before Edgewater knew what had happened, it had been wiped off the map of Chicago as a separate entity and combined with Uptown as "Uptown"* Community Area #3. Though never stamped with official approval from the City's planning department, the University of Chicago map came to be widely used, unofficially, in locating Chicago's communities.

For the next five decades, public utilities, downtown banks and mortgage houses, church organizations, philanthropic bodies, the print and electronic media, government officials from out of town and others who dealt with Chicago's local communities were seldom able to trace Edgewater. Their long-distance view was too remote to recognize Edgewater's community newspapers, the local hospital and the various Protestant churches which used Edgewater in their titles, the neighborhood telephone directories, whenever they parenthetically acknowledged Edgewater's existence, or the presence of the Edgewater Golf Club (which was finally sold and converted into a public park in the 1970s). Their faraway view also

---

*Hereafter, whenever the reference is to Community Area #3, "Uptown" is put within quotation marks. References to the actual Uptown community, the smaller area, do not carry quotation marks.

failed to appreciate the community significance in the name of the Edgewater Beach Hotel which was finally torn down in the late 1960s and replaced in the early 1970s by three apartment skyscrapers called, not unexpectedly, Edgewater Plaza.

Edgewater Submerged

From distant towers downtown, it was not difficult to overlook Edgewater. Looking north, the viewers could see Loyola University, Illinois' largest private university, located in East Rogers Park by the lake. Then there were the large insurance headquarters, banks, and savings and loan associations which could be found in Uptown. Finally, there were the residents in the high-rises on Sheridan Road, who were simply seen as living along the lakefront. But somewhere in between, if one searched more carefully, one would discover Edgewater.

During the decades immediately following World War II, the City's preoccupation with Uptown derailed Edgewater's ambition to restore its own identity. As a shocked Uptown saw its prewar boom collapse, the signs of community decay and economic depression could be seen almost everywhere, in both its commercial and residential sections. To no one's surprise, City agencies, in the 1950s and 1960s, steered their attention to Uptown's housing deterioration, its abandoned buildings, its deepening poverty, its double-shift schools, its enlarged skid row, and its demoralized business district. The Mayor's Committee on New Residents, the Department of Urban Renewal, the Chicago Committee on Urban Opportunity and the Chicago Model Cities Program, to name only four city agencies, moved in with physical improvements and social programs to upgrade the community. During these decades, however, the City's high priorities for Uptown ignored Edgewater's urgent claim to its own identity. Edgewater simply was not on the City's agenda.

In fact, keeping Edgewater invisible and submerging its neighborhoods under the "Uptown" umbrella, for statistical and other purposes, made the Uptown portion of Community Area #3 look better than it actually was. Associating the strengths of these northerly neighborhoods with Uptown's nearly overwhelming decline was seen as a badly needed support for Uptown's revitalization. As federally-funded programs, such as Model Cities, gave priority to mixed income areas, more and more of Edgewater was gathered into Uptown which had become the target of one federal program after another. Thus planners concerned with deteriorating conditions so visibly concentrated in Uptown did not hesitate to move its northern boundary farther and farther into Edgewater, so that Edgewater's remaining residents were gradually left with less and less urban territory to claim as their own.

In these two decades, then, it was "Uptown," as Chicago's port of entry for Appalachian whites and American Indians, that caught the mass media's attention. National magazines carried feature articles. Books were published. "Uptown" Community Area #3 was in; Edgewater was out. Ignored by all, Edgewater was suffering from pernicious anonymity.

Despite Edgewater's continuing struggle over the years to gain recognition for itself and for the right to help outline its own boundaries, seldom did its concerns catch the attention of downtown bureaucracies. One pastor recalled his twenty years of experience in these words:

> We always discovered, after the maps had been printed or published, what the U.S. Post Office, Model Cities, public aid, police department or fire department boundaries were going to be. We rarely received advance notice.
>
> In our search for recognition as Edgewater, it seems that whenever we took one step forward, we also took two backwards. When we tried to help the downtown decision-makers set service district boundaries, we found ourselves so entangled in red tape that we felt lucky when we escaped their forms, regulations, procedures, clearances, guidelines, and, last but not least, "regular channels."
>
> The district administrators were accustomed to shifting boundaries and naming their districts to suit their own convenience and to fit their own purposes, which might or might not coincide with the community's. We were always at their mercy. They acted as if they, and they alone, had the divine right to determine where and how services to our community would be delivered, even if we did not want them!

Edgewater Threatened

When it came to police protection, Edgewater by 1981 was divided between two different Chicago police districts, with both headquarters located *outside* the Edgewater community. As far as the U.S. Post Office was concerned, Edgewater's mail was delivered via two zip codes, 60640 and 60660, which embraced adjoining communities as well.

Political boundaries also help to preserve or weaken a community's unity. The Chicago City Council had fifty aldermen, each representing a ward. But Edgewater's political influence was diffused among four wards, though a clear majority of the community's voters did live in a single ward, the 48th. In addition, Edgewater's political influence was split between two legislative districts which sent representatives to the Illinois General Assembly in Springfield. On the other side of the ledger, Edgewater fell entirely within the 9th U.S. Congressional District. All eleven public schools educating the youngsters of Edgewater were included in the Chicago Board of Education's District 24.

Edgewater's pursuit of its own political identity came to another crossroads in 1981 as the redistricting of the city wards and legislative districts took place to respond to the findings of the decennial U.S. Census.

In Edgewater a seasoned youth counsellor, who for several decades had been watching the drawing and re-drawing of the boundaries of governmental service districts, said:

> The Balkanization of administrative boundaries was almost as destructive of the Uptown and Edgewater communities as any expressway that might have been built through their center.

The gradual incorporation of Edgewater into "Uptown," in the citizenry's subconsciousness, was made easier by recognizable similarities between the two communities. Slightly on the defensive, a real estate broker said:

> The two communities do, you know, share a lake together and miles of lakefront park. Facing the lake stands a spectacular row of residential high-rises which remind me of Miami and Rio de Janeiro. Both communities have housing which is much older and densely built.

And don't forget the apartment hotels with their furnished but obsolete kitchenettes. For decades they have been dragging each community down because no one knows what to do with them—except to turn them into halfway houses, sheltered care facilities or flophouses.

And then, most important of all, there is the corridor which runs through the center of Uptown. Here the same elevated line, Broadway Avenue and Sheridan Road serve both communities. Looking through a telescope from the Loop office of the Chicago Title and Trust Company, you see only the similarities; the differences become blurred. Or if you drive along the lake and look inland, all you notice would be the resemblances. You never see what lies behind the high-rises. Only when you come and trudge the streets or drive a car through Uptown and Edgewater do you begin to notice the variations.

The Corridor in Edgewater and Uptown: The Dissimilarities

The most striking difference visible to the eye between the two communities is the retail, banking and transportation core which dominates Uptown. There is nothing like it in Edgewater whose visual image, despite its commercial strips, is predominantly residential. Augmenting the business character of Uptown is the presence of Combined Insurance Company, which employs 1,500 workers. Kemper Insurance Company, Uptown's other large employer, moved to the suburbs in the late 1960s; its large building then became the international headquarters for the Ecumenical Institute, a world-wide religious organization which sponsors social and community renewal projects in thirty-two countries.

During the 1960s and 1970s, Uptown acquired a second, but unwelcome distinction: the scarring presence of large parcels of vacant land on which once had stood residential buildings. Now conspicuously absent, hundreds of these multi-family apartments were either devoured by fire or simply abandoned by their owners. These dangerous and dilapidated buildings were eventually demolished by wrecking crews hired by the City, burdening Uptown with nearly 300 acres of forsaken wasteland.

Edgewater's unmistakable feature is its mile-long canyon, along Sheridan Road and next to Lake Michigan, lined with residential high-rises on both sides of the narrow boulevard and dominating the skyline. The tallest is a triangular tower which shoots up fifty-five stories and contains 728 condominiums. Along this section of the lakefront, high-rise apartments stand directly at the lake's edge, one of the few stretches of Chicago's twenty-seven miles of lakefront where the public has no free and open access. Most of the mansions built early in the century were torn down to make room for these skyscrapers. In the years following World War II, developers took advantage of the Lake Shore Drive extension to construct this spectacular wall of high-rise buildings not only along Sheridan Road in Edgewater but also further south along Marine Drive in Uptown. According to one reliable estimate, this three-mile section of Edgewater and Uptown fronting the lake saw nearly $1 billion worth of new residential construction in the three decades following the close of World War II.

Middle class families who rent these apartments face the lake visually and emotionally, their backs to Edgewater. They are separated from the stable neighborhoods of West Edgewater by the corridor, its elevated line, and the Broadway business strip.

While this dramatic residential development solidified Edgewater's own fiscal base and enlarged its political influence downtown, a new set of community concerns emerged. The high densities aggravated traffic congestion and the shortage of parking spots for autos. Residents began to demand additional recreational space and more direct access to the lake.

By 1981 Sheridan Road's concentrated housing, together with the residential compactness along Winthrop and Kenmore, made Edgewater, especially its eastern half, the most densely populated community in Chicago. In that year Edgewater had a population of 59,000. As a whole, Edgewater is a tightly built-up community, even in its western, low-rise neighborhoods where vacant parcels of land are simply non-existent. Thus no one was surprised in the late 1970s when the Edgewater Community Council organized a not-for-profit corporation, called Urban Programs North, to undertake housing rehabilitation, while Uptown set up its own not-for-profit corporation, but for local economic and commercial redevelopment.

Edgewater Consciousness

By 1960 Edgewater's distinctiveness had laid the groundwork for the "territorial imperative" to make its influence felt. Residents could now identify with Edgewater as a separate community that they were proud to call their own. In that year, with initiative from the ministers, priests and rabbis of Edgewater's religious institutions, the Edgewater Community Council (ECC) was organized for this purpose:

> To promote the physical, social, aesthetic and civic development of that area of the City of Chicago known as the Edgewater area and to prevent the physical, social, aesthetic and civic deterioration of said Edgewater area.

Those words, taken from the ECC's original charter, indicated the institutional leadership's sensitivity to, and self-consciousness about, Edgewater's suppressed identity; their determination to safeguard Edgewater from the epidemic of blight which had infected Uptown; and their hope that Edgewater's growing fears and concerns about its own future would be resolved with greater success than Uptown's. The clergy took the lead, but the laity soon carried the ball. The formation of ECC provoked the "great library battle" which lasted more than a decade. Rogers Park had its own public library; so did Uptown. But Edgewater was bereft. Under ECC's leadership the community rallied time and again trying to persuade the Chicago Public Library board to open a permanent branch in Edgewater. Finally, ground was broken in 1974 for a new building. It was a double victory: the community had its own library, and the library bore the name of Edgewater.

Around 1972, the ECC acquired a new board member, Leroy Blommaert. He served three terms as ECC president from 1974 through 1976. Almost single-handedly, Blommaert made Edgewater's identity a one-man crusade among newspaper reporters, block clubs, elected officials and even the ECC board of directors themselves, demanding that all of them give Edgewater its due:

> The thrust of the Edgewater promotion is twofold and can be summed up in the following statements: Edgewater is a distinct

Chicago community; Edgewater is a desirable Chicago Community. The two elements are distinguishable but they are at times so closely related that the distinction becomes blurred. To the extent that we promote Edgewater as a desirable community, we also promote it as a distinct community.

Young, aggressive and self-confident, Blommaert made a lasting impact.

The territorial imperative, which Blommaert asserted, led Edgewater's business, religious and community leaders to a self-defense strategy through which they would accent Edgewater's unique advantages and dissimilarities to Uptown. They sought to retain the middle income families dribbling away to other city and suburban communities and hoped to attract similar families wherever a vacancy occurred. These objectives were especially important to the Winthrop-Kenmore corridor. If stable, upwardly-mobile renters kept by-passing Edgewater because they thought they would be moving into "Uptown," the typical corridor landlord would be in fiscal trouble. To keep from going broke, some landlords would lower their rental standards, postpone routine maintenance on multi-family buildings and accept the first tenants who showed up as long as they could pay the rent. Next would come poor management of the property, irregular payment of rents by tenants, evictions, rent strikes, and overcrowded apartments. A veteran policeman described the corridor's real estate market as follows:

> The corridor was the soft underbelly of Edgewater. The very forces which badly bruised Uptown's center were now creeping into Edgewater via the Winthrop-Kenmore corridor. Edgewater's piece of the corridor was now as vulnerable as Uptown's earlier. As apartment buildings were demolished in Uptown, their refugees headed up the Edgewater corridor. The hard-core unemployed, welfare families with a single parent, alcoholics, former patients of state hospitals for the mentally ill and others began filling up Edgewater's apartment hotels.
>
> You know the result. Some Edgewater owners gave up and abandoned their properties. Other buildings were gutted by deadly fires. Winthrop Avenue today [1981] is strewn with large boarded-up buildings. They look ominous.

Housing deterioration, crime and prostitution are not part of Edgewater's future; they're already present, disgracing the corridor.

To safeguard Edgewater's individuality, Community Council leaders determined to free themselves from the "Uptown" image which was being foisted upon them by politicians, bankers, newspaper and television editors, urban consultants and church staffs who were based downtown. This view of "Uptown" was clouding Edgewater's future by weakening its ability to deal massively and effectively with the crime, deterioration and arson creeping into Edgewater. Why? Understandably, City Hall had riveted its attention on solving Uptown's more serious problems. Instead of taking individualized approaches to Edgewater and Uptown, the downtown bureaucracy lumped them together in its planning for "Uptown." But Edgewater's social conditions and physical dilapidation were not as serious as was the situation in Uptown's section of the corridor. Would the same approach be effective for both? A board member of the Edgewater Community Council offered an answer:

> We had to oppose any solution to Uptown's problems which simply exported them to Edgewater using the corridor as the conduit.

> Uptown's disintegration was finally halted. It had reached bottom and had nowhere to go but up. And Uptown is in fact coming back to life. Revitalizing its retail and commercial center and finding investors willing to build on vacant land are planning and developmental strageies not appropriate to Edgewater. It needs, instead, to rebuild public confidence in the corridor so that physical improvement and social rehabilitation can proceed more rapidly.

> If Edgewater succeeds, who will be the chief beneficiary? Uptown. The upgrading of the Edgewater section of the corridor will encourage investors to take the risk and build new housing and commercial buildings on the vacant acres along Winthrop and Kenmore in Uptown.

A former board member of the Uptown Chicago Commission corroborated this point of view:

The emergence of Edgewater helped Uptown fix its own identity, narrow its boundaries more precisely and thus give it a smaller territory to worry about. Uptown could now concentrate its attention on solutions to its own special problems instead of being distracted by every new federal and city program which invaded Uptown from somewhere on high. Uptown's leaders had spread themselves too thin for several decades, thus diffusing their impact. Now they could give prime attention to reviving Uptown's mid-section, the troubled transportation and commercial center.

Probably the most fundamental difference between Edgewater and Uptown was a matter of attitude. The view in Uptown was that the urban damage had already been done. How would Uptown now repair and rebuild its central commercial core? The view in Edgewater was that it had not yet happened to them. What was an accomplished condition in Uptown had started to undermine Edgewater. Could Edgewater halt the tide of blight and keep from being overwhelmed by it? Any planning which neglected this diversity of perspective was headed for failure.

Some Roadblocks

Countervailing forces operate not only in economics but also in community redevelopment. Some ten years after the Edgewater Community Council was formed, another community organization emerged, with a staff and budget more than double that of the Edgewater Community Council. But staff size and finances were not as important as territoriality. What mattered was that the new group, the Organization of the North East (ONE, for short), proposed to speak on behalf of "Uptown," using the troublesome boundaries of Community Area #3. Once again Edgewater was being overshadowed—only this time by another community organization. One of the early ONE organizers explained:

> Our real interest was Uptown. We came to help Uptown help itself; to organize it so that real changes would occur; and to empower the poor so that the City's urban renewal wouldn't dare to push them out.
>
> I knew where Uptown was, but as an out-of-towner I didn't know its boundaries. I looked them up in the *Local Community Fact Book* which carried the U.S. census data by community area. Only

later did we realize that with those "Uptown" boundaries we had also inherited Edgewater; and that Edgewater was not simply another neighborhood but a real community. In speaking for the community, we found ourselves either straddling two communities, Uptown and Edgewater, or trying to persuade Edgewater's residents and institutions to come under our "Uptown" umbrella.

Brooks Miller, one of the original members of ONE and head of Hull House's Uptown Center, explained how ONE was started in Uptown where his community center is located:

> At the beginning of the seventies Uptown had many of the same problems that it faces today. High crime along many streets, redlining by area financial institutions, and slum landlords milking their buildings for all they are worth. At that time there was no local organization that the people of Uptown could use to attack genuine community issues. Other north side communities such as Rogers Park... and Edgewater had some type of citizens council.
>
> We formed an issue and action oriented group that originally called itself Uptown Special Projects. It was not until the convention was held... in 1973 that the name the Organization of the North East was adopted. For at least the first two years Uptown Center Hull House provided the structure, received the funding, and handled the bookkeeping for the fledgling coalition. And when ONE encountered tough times, which were frequent in the early days, Hull House provided the money for the organization to get through.

ONE's objective was to create a single community by mobilizing residents around "crises" such as the one depicted on page 37.

During this decade, competition between ONE and the Edgewater Community Council ebbed and flowed, depending on the issue. Whenever a genteel tug-of-war would ensue, organizational rivalry and jealousy were the explanations most frequently given. However, what troubled Edgewater residents most, whether they fully understood it or not, was that Edgewater was somehow being eclipsed. For in peddling its version of what constituted "Uptown" or in trying to make one community of "Edgewater-Uptown," ONE, intentionally or not, befogged the Edgewater identity. The upshot of this rivalry, paradoxically, was that ONE's appearance

UPTOWN-EDGEWATER RESIDENTS:
BEWARE!
OUR COMMUNITY IS BURNING!

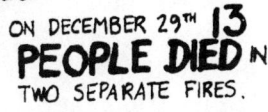

ON DECEMBER 29TH **13 PEOPLE DIED** IN TWO SEPARATE FIRES.

SINCE LAST JUNE OVER **200 FIRES** HAVE OCCURED IN EDGEWATER-UPTOWN, MANY IN BUILDINGS OWNED BY THE AREA'S WORST SLUMLORDS.

IF YOU LIVE IN OR NEAR ONE OF THESE BUILDINGS

YOUR LIFE COULD BE IN DANGER!

EACH DOT REPRESENTS THE LOCATION OF A FIRE SINCE JUNE

Stop the spread of arson!

COME TO A **PUBLIC MEETING** SPONSORED BY ONE

INVITED GUESTS: **SAMUEL NOLAN** (PUBLIC SAFETY DIRECTOR) **RICHARD ALBRECHT** (FIRE COM.) **ROBERT BRZECZEK** (POLICE SUPERINTENDENT)

TUESDAY, JANUARY 29th, 7:30 PM
ST. THOMAS OF CANTERBURY CHURCH, 4827 N KENMORE

one ORGANIZATION OF THE NORTH EAST 1105 W. LAWRENCE   CHICAGO, ILL. 60640   312-769-3232 RM 202 on the Edgewater horizon served, in the long run, not to weaken ECC, as many feared, but to galvanize it into action. Not wanting Edgewater played down, its residents were now more ready to align themselves with Edgewater and its own community organization. By 1981 the Edgewater Community Council had more dues-paying members than it did in the early 1970s when ONE began organizing in Edgewater and Uptown.

Without intending to do so, the rising self-consciousness of Edgewater and the growing strength of its Community Council challenged the credibility of ONE's claim to speak on behalf of Edgewater, even though ONE had by 1981 become the largest (in the number of staff) and the biggest (in the size of its budget) community organization on Chicago's north side. Besides conflicting claims over territorial representation, the rivalry between the two organizations extended to competition over credit for an achievement, over resources (from foundations, businesses, and churches), and over leadership (the pool of potential community leaders is limited). An Edgewater resident who had been wooed both by ONE and by the Council for her participation and loyalty summed up the situation:

> ONE is very attractive. It has uncovered some dedicated community leaders. It has a flair for the dramatic and a genius for publicity. It moves quickly and at times effectively. When it comes to showmanship in dramatizing an issue, real or ill-conceived, ONE understands melodrama. When it comes to issues, ONE is a revolving door, because the "issues" seem to change so frequently. It's *ONE* crisis after another, if you will pardon the pun.
>
> The Council is more staid, conservative in style and approach. It is slower to move but when it does, it has staying power—like a bulldog. The Council is also good at publicity. When you consider the smallness of its staff, it's amazing how much the Council accomplishes each year. You can take your choice: the tortoise or the hare: the Council or ONE.

Is this community activist correct in her assessment? Only the next decade will tell.

Some Unexpected Developments

Everyone expected the Edgewater Community Council to mobilize local residents, clergy and businessmen in order to revive Edgewater and to defend itself against all enemies, foreign and domestic. And ECC did that. But it was the unintended consequences, which ECC organizers did not foresee, that did even more to keep Edgewater's morale high and increase its grass-roots membership during the 1960s and 1970s. Among its residents, Edgewater was not simply a tract of land any longer but also a state of mind.

● The first of these consequences was the awakening of Edgewater's neighborhoods which, in size, were usually as large as a parish or an elementary school district. Several block clubs appeared so that by 1981, ECC officers could identify thirteen separate neighborhoods. Five of these neighborhoods used Edgewater in the name of their association: Edgewater Glen Association, Edgewater Residents Together in Action, Edgewater Beach Improvement Association, Northwest Edgewater Neighbors Association and North Central Edgewater. Most of the neighborhood organizations were actively affiliated with the Council; some even organized with ECC's aid. This intermediate layer of associations—between the residents on the one hand and ECC on the other—gave ECC a solid public platform from which to speak and provided an effective, two-way medium for communicating information about issues facing Edgewater.

● The re-awakening of Edgewater had a second unintended consequence. Loyola University began reconsidering its posture vis-à-vis the surrounding community. Situated on the lakefront in Rogers Park immediately north of Devon Ave., the northern boundary of Edgewater, the campus had historically associated itself with Rogers Park. The University's community orientation was north and west, but its landscaping was something else. Loyola's early classroom and residential buildings were erected to face the lake, awaiting the day when the lake would be filled in and a frontage road would run past the University's front door. Extending such a road would have added several badly needed acres to Loyola's land-starved campus. But that day has not yet come, even after seventy years.

Looking in the westerly direction, but still in Rogers Park, the University maintained strong ties with St. Ignatius parish, also staffed by Jesuit priests and brothers, two blocks to the west. During the 1930s and 1940s, this parish was recognized throughout the Chicago metropolitan area as the model of a thriving religious institution. But in the decades following World War II, the parish was caught up in the exodus of younger families, the influx of new ethnic and religious populations, the increasing number of elderly residents, and finally, shifting Jesuit priorities. During these years, the University's enrollment exploded geometrically, flooding St. Ignatius parish with a temporary and transient population and intensifying the parish's doldrums. The upshot was an uneasy relationship between parish and campus, not unlike the "town and gown" tensions which had visited urban universities elsewhere. University linkages to its parish community were not easy to accomplish. In 1978, for example, among the University's top forty-six officials (from assistant dean to president), only eight were residents of Rogers Park or Edgewater; and six of these were Jesuits who lived in their community residence located on campus.

As Loyola's enrollment multiplied, many more students began living south of Devon Avenue in Edgewater—in fraternity houses, apartment hotels, University-owned residence halls, and private residences. The owners of blighted, obsolete, hard-to-rent properties also welcomed the apartment-hunting collegians and their monthly rents. Through this student experience, the problems associated with the Winthrop-Kenmore corridor—purse snatchings, assault, stolen and abandoned cars, burnt-out buildings, and drug peddling—began showing up regularly on the University's own agenda. A Loyola professor explained:

> For half a century the University had regarded itself as located in Rogers Park. I could see no appreciation that Loyola's future was also tied to Edgewater's. Eventually, the University's leadership came to realize that its southern flank was exposed and that the blight being transported up the corridor would eventually be unloaded on the campus. That new understanding meant that Loyola, for all practical purposes, considered itself part of Edgewater as well.

How would the University respond? The appearance of the Edgewater Community Council alerted Loyola officials that they now had a viable, community-based outlet for dealing with their concerns about the social environment of the University's southern edge. Thus the Council provided a safe passage for the University's efforts to deal with rising fears about the future of Edgewater. Without seeming to threaten the community, the University could provide financial support, could recruit faculty and administrative personnel for ECC membership, its committees and board of directors and could encourage students to volunteer in community projects. Not surprisingly, in 1980 the University finally acknowledged that its Lake Shore Campus also lay in Edgewater. In publishing its official map, Loyola University for the first time dropped the southern edge of its campus below Devon Avenue and embraced two blocks of Edgewater which included the upper end of the Winthrop-Kenmore corridor.

● In another development in the 1970s, the cliff dwellers who inhabited the newer high-rises packed along Sheridan Road began to take a second look at Edgewater. An old-time resident narrated the change:

> Had you asked me fifteen years ago where I lived I would have said "on Sheridan Road" or "on the lake up north." You'd never hear me reply, "in Edgewater." Having turned our backs on the city behind us, my neighbors and I embraced the lake instead, psychologically. In splendid isolation, we were oriented to Sheridan Road and Lake Michigan—cut off from the Edgewater mainland, as it were, on our private island.
>
> Ten years ago, we began hearing more about Edgewater. But the residents who were moving into the newly-built apartments down the street had the same fixation about the lake that we did. Some of us did join the Edgewater Community Council. But not many; it was tokenism.
>
> But five years ago, were we shaken up! We learned that our tight little island existed only in our imagination. What had happened? I can only give you my experience. The east-to-west streets across which we walked, to take the elevated downtown or to get to Broadway Avenue where we shopped, changed overnight. It was frightening. The lady who lives in the apartment above me was knocked down and her purse taken. Drunks stumbled down the street, pleading for a quarter. More bars opened up, catering to "winos" and transients. Streetwalkers showed up in gaudy pant

suits and paraded down the street, looking to be picked up. My wife was really bothered about them, more than I was. What did we do? We stopped walking and used our auto as an "armored car" even on a bright sunny day, to drive to Broadway two blocks away. Instead of taking the elevated train, we rode the Sheridan Road bus.

As we heard horror stories about the Winthrop-Kenmore corridor, we learned that the leaders of the Edgewater Community Council came mostly from the neighborhoods west of Broadway. They were doing *our* job for us. We also met property owners who lived on Winthrop and Kenmore. They were worried—just as we were. And they were improving their properties! They were rooting for their neighborhood organization and for ECC as well.

Do you want to ask me now where I live?

The fears of east and west Edgewater, about the corridor lying between them, began to reunite the community. The reunion was a three-way combination which also included the renters and owners living along Winthrop and Kenmore.

● What could not have been foreseen was the investment revolution which overtook Sheridan Road during the 1970s. That was the decade of the condominium. Suddenly, thousands of apartment renters found themselves compelled to buy their apartment as a condominium if they wanted to remain residents of Sheridan Road at the lake. Most did not want to move and had no alternative but to invest. What once had been a high-rise haven for renters became a street of individual property owners.

The switch from renting to owning had side effects which were unprecedented. Typically, a large apartment building serves as a refuge for renters who seek privacy and who shun the responsibility of being neighbors. They find the idealized isolation they seek, paradoxically, in an apartment cubicle rented within a densely populated skyscraper. But now that Sheridan Road residents owned their individual properties, they quickly sensed that they were also neighbors; that the policy-setting meetings of the condominium association were devoted to concerns which all shared. Their highrise of condominiums had been converted, to everyone's astonishment, into a vertical neighborhood. Having taken the first step, becoming a neighborhood, the condo proprietors began taking the next step, identifying their interest with Edgewater's.

Whether the living area is horizontal or vertical, the experience is that the higher the proportion of property owners, the more likely it is that a neighborhood will thrive. The horizontal neighborhoods already know this to be true. Now the vertical, high-rise neighborhoods, peopled with condominium owners, are finding it out for themselves.

● The influx of newcomers into Edgewater, primarily into the corridor but also along Sheridan Road and in the western neighborhoods as well, helped coalesce a community sense of pride about Edgewater's acceptance of racial and ethnic change. On any Sunday, Bible classes and church services are conducted in Korean, Greek, Armenian, Spanish, Rumanian, Japanese, Chinese, Filipino, Hebrew or Cambodian. The large supermarkets best reflect the changing ethnic and racial character of Edgewater—both in the many-hued complexions of shoppers and the variety of ethnic foods sold.

Most schools in Edgewater, public and private, enrolled substantial numbers of Hispanic, Oriental and black students. For example, Swift, a public elementary school, had a student body which was 47 percent black, 18 percent East Asian and 24 percent Hispanic in 1981. In Chicago or any of its suburbs, it would be hard to find another community which had as large an entry of blacks, unaccompanied by racial violence. This in-migration trickled into Edgewater in the 1960s, becoming a continuous stream, especially into the corridor, in the 1970s.

The Edgewater community was willing, up to a point, to accept the growing diversity of class, race and ethnicity. Their accommodation to these social changes was—to the newcomers—a positive sign. But in recent years the pace of change accelerated. The result was a surging fear of an inundation so great and so overwhelming that the corridor might become the city's newest concentration of deep-rooted poverty. Furthermore, would the corridor's depressing social conditions eventually burst into the adjoining areas of Edgewater? Concerns for reverse racial segregation were widespread—and real.

The most discouraging, pervasive fear was that of serious crime, bodily harm and rape. While the *incidence* of serious crime in the corridor rose slowly, though steadily, the *perception* of unsafe streets escalated dramatically. As the panicky atmosphere settled in, stable families with children were less attracted to move into the community. The corridor's landlords not only deferred maintenance on their properties but also stopped screening tenants, filling up the apartments with any occupant who showed up with the rent money.

Senn High School, serving both Edgewater and Uptown, undoubtedly houses the most diverse student enrollment of any secondary school in the city. An Edgewater parent who is active in the high school's Parent-Teacher Association conveyed her sense of community achievement, saying:

> Senn High School is a teen-age miniature of the United Nations. Thirty-four languages are spoken. Hundreds of Senn's 2,300 students are foreign-born. It's doing a better job of balancing racial and ethnic tensions than does the UN itself. Having had our share of racial and ethnic hostility, we could teach the UN a few things. Am I proud that Senn is located in Edgewater!

The Year That Was

Edgewater's re-emergence as a community—now finally visible to the entire city—can be pinpointed with some precision. The year was 1978, twelve dramatic months during which the community's residents challenged the city's political and planning establishment —and won—without a bitter aftermath.

In 1978 Loyola University's political science department issued its academic "endorsement" regarding the presence of two separate communities by publishing Jane E. Ratcliffe's study: *A Community in Transition: The Edgewater Community in Chicago.* One homeowner reacted to the study by saying:

> We knew all along that Edgewater was here, struggling to survive. Now, I hope, downtown's wheelers and dealers will stop ignoring us and recognize our existence.

Several months later the University's political science department

Edgewater Threatened

issued a second study, this time by Elizabeth Warren, entitled *Chicago's Uptown: Public Policy, Neighborhood Decay and Citizen Action in an Urban Community.* Once again, the study reinforced the growing conviction that there were indeed *two* communities and that the University of Chicago social scientists had erred decades ago in erasing Edgewater from their map of Chicago.

In the same year the voters of the 48th Ward, which represents more than half of Edgewater, elected an alderman who not only lived in Edgewater but had also served as president of the Edgewater Community Council. The Ward's four previous aldermen had come from its Uptown section. The new alderman, Marion Kennedy Volini, ran as a "community candidate," and had to buck the regular Democratic political organization in order to defeat its handpicked candidate who was a resident of Uptown.

During the 1960s the bulk of the voters in the 48th Ward, with its northern boundary at Bryn Mawr Avenue and its southern border at Irving Park Road, lived in Uptown. But after the decennial redistricting that took place in 1972, the boundaries of the 48th Ward were moved northwards nearly a mile so that the great majority of its voters now lived in Edgewater. The larger part of Uptown lay in the 46th Ward. The redistribution of the 48th Ward's political power reflected not only a decline in Uptown's proportion of the ward's eligible voters but also the politcal independence of voters whose consciousness as residents of the Edgewater community had been raised. By 1978 both Republican and Democratic Committeemen of the 48th Ward were property-owning residents of Edgewater.

In 1978 the Edgewater Community Council had the most active year in its eighteen-year history, a year crammed with highly visible and dramatic events. (See illustration on page 45.) During those twelve months, the Council, with the full support of the new alderman, did such an extraordinary job of mobilizing thousands of residents, especially those who lived in the Sheridan Road skyscrapers, that City Hall itself was shaken up. The issue which brought this about was a controversial proposal that federal subsidies be used to build a high-rise which would house low-income families on Sheridan Road. The housing project had the support of the Mayor of Chicago, the Commissioner of Planning, the 48th Ward Democratic Committeeman, and the Illinois Housing Devel-

Edgewater Threatened

opment Authority. While public hearings were taking place, an inexpensive lapel sticker appeared, the handiwork of some unknown designer. Before long, hundreds of protestors began to sport this sticker:

Faced with a community-wide uprising, City Hall capitulated. The Chicago Plan Commission vetoed the proposal. There was no doubt in anyone's mind that Edgewater not only had made its voice heard but also had earned the right to a partnership role in future City Hall decisions affecting the Community.

Urged on by these events, the board of directors of the Edgewater Community Council in 1978 drafted a "position statement" and approved it unanimously early in the following year:

> It has been long-standing ECC policy to increase awareness and recognition of Edgewater as a distinct community among both resident and non-resident alike. Because of various forces working at cross purposes to this policy, it becomes desirable from time to time to re-affirm Edgewater's separate identity....
>
> Edgewater is an historical community in its own right, separate and distinct from Rogers Park on the north and Uptown on the south....
>
> Edgewater is not the southern part of something called Rogers Park/Edgewater, nor is it the northern part of something called Edgewater/Uptown, nor is it a neighborhood within a Community Area #3 ["Uptown"] as depicted in the various editions of the *Local Community Fact Book*....

The Council's emphasis and insistence that Edgewater is a distinct Chicago community does not represent a "go it alone" posture or an unwillingness to work with groups in neighborhood communities or a belief that Edgewater does not share problems and prospects with Rogers Park to the north and Uptown to the south.

The council then asked "that the media, and in particular the Lerner Press, properly identify Edgewater residents as Edgewater residents, Edgewater happenings as Edgewater happenings, and Edgewater locations as Edgewater locations."

Even the downtown mapmakers were impressed. When the City's Planning Department in 1978 first identified the city's twenty "interim neighborhood strategy areas" for the expenditure of $114,000,000 of federal Community Development Block Grant funds, lo and behold, there were separate maps for the Edgewater and Uptown planning areas. When the North Side Real Estate Board in 1979 issued twenty-one Community Guides to "Our Town's... north side neighborhoods," Uptown and Edgewater were each singled out separately on the map. When in 1980, First Federal of Chicago, the largest savings and loan association in Illinois, distributed several hundred thousand copies of its map of ninety-three Chicago "neighborhoods," Edgewater was one of them.

The most important milestone in Edgewater's unrelenting pursuit of an identity was reached in mid-1980 when Martin R. Murphy, the Commissioner of Planning for the City of Chicago, wrote Robert Remer, president of the Edgewater Community Council as follows:

> ...the Edgewater Community Area will be identified as a distinct Community Area in future editions of appropriate city maps. This newly designated Community Area will also be incorporated in the collection and the aggregation of Community Area statistics.

After fifty years, the University of Chicago map would finally be altered. Edgewater was now on an "official" map. Since Edgewater had been there all along, alive and well, the decision of geographers in the Planning Department to put Edgewater back on the map of Chicago became a symbolic victory for local residents. They now realized that their sphere of influence did reach downtown.

On urban landscapes everywhere, there thrive neighborhoods and communities which go unrecognized or are ignored—by the mass media or on official or unofficial maps. The story of Edgewater's failures—and ultimate success—in pursuit of its identity is a reminder that the "invisible community," like the "invisible man," gasps for identity, for communication, and for the chance to be recognized and appreciated. As a community gains recognition from the larger world outside and earns the respect of its peers in communities elsewhere in the city, such a distinction becomes a powerful force in community revitalization. Edgewater's history is a reminder that while the road to renewing and rebuilding a city is strewn with obstacles, they can be overcome.

4

Thirteen Neighborhoods But a Single Community

Historically, Edgewater's re-emergence as a community can be traced to the revival of its neighborhoods. For between the individual households of families, singles or elderly couples and the community as a whole, there lies an intermediate layer, the neighborhood. Here, in the interaction between individuals and their neighbors, the larger community ultimately discovers both its character and its impetus for action.

Defining the Neighborhood

The social fabric of the city is most clearly evident at the level of a neighborhood, an enclave much smaller in breadth than the community and usually the size of an elementary school's attendance area, a Catholic parish or the vicinity immediately adjoining a business strip. Neighborhood boundaries can further be defined by a railroad, an expressway, a river, a public park, or a cemetery. This terrain then *becomes* a neighborhood through its social environment; through face-to-face relationships, through the goings-on inside such local institutions as the school building, church or synagogue; through the talk of mothers as they watch their children at the playground; through the exchange at the laundromat, corner tavern, fraternal lodge, pre-school center or supermarket; through activities, such as a scout troop, school PTA or mothers' club, school safety patrol, little league baseball, baby-sitting co-op, bingo games, garage sales, block parties or the weekly church bulletin;

through events which are shared and celebrated with relatives and neighbors, such as a graduation, baptism, bar mitzvah, birthday, funeral, wedding, holiday, ethnic commemoration or class reunion; and, finally, through intermingling service areas, such as the police beat, political precinct, mail delivery route or census tract. As everyone knows, the arrival of the age of the automobile affected such older neighborhoods, usually adversely. Car ownership accelerated mobility, de-emphasizing the importance of neighborhood boundaries as being "within walking distance."

What is noteworthy is that while Edgewater's neighborhoods each carry their own ethnic and religious histories, they survive today, but not as revivals of some older ethnic domain. As we move closer to the twenty-first century, they represent some of the *new* urban neighborhoods where home owners strain their ingenuity and pocketbooks to prevail in an urban society which has yet to appreciate fully the neighborhood's importance. The new urban neighborhood, now enduring growing pains, is not ethnic, nor is it based on class and race, as were, after World War II, the suburban neighborhoods populated by young couples bearing children. The new urban neighborhood welcomes the upwardly-mobile, whether working or middle class, married or single, who are attracted by the diverse opportunities available in the city's labor market and who are urbane in life-style, relishing the cosmopolitanism of the metropolis. Seeking the excitement of the urban place, they own homes or condominiums and want roots for themselves. Desiring access to excellence for school-age sons and daughters, parents desperately search for confidence in the local schools, whether public or private, as places where standards of behavior and moral values will be caught as well as taught.

The Edgewater neighborhoods west of Broadway Avenue fit this portrait of the new urban neighborhood. They are ethnically and socially diverse, racially integrated and multi-religious. Generally family centered, they are peopled by tradesmen and college graduates, many of whom own their own residences. Parents who decide to stay in the city so that their children may benefit from urban hubbub find such a neighborhood especially attractive because it also offers safety, privacy and a measure of tranquility. Finally, they can afford financially to live in one.

Defining the Community

Broader than any one neighborhood and weaving several of them together through common goals is the community. It is closer to the size of a public high school or police district, a political ward, or a postal zone. It is large or wealthy enough to support a bank, hospital, community newspaper, shopping center, public library, secondary school, Kiwanis Club, one or more movie theaters, American Legion Post, police station, recreational center, several restaurants, a park with a fieldhouse, and the many activities generated by such organizations. As in the case of the neighborhood, "auto-mobility" has also tended to make the community's edges somewhat vague.

At the city level, elected public officials, the public utilities, planning commissions, mass media, advertising and public relations firms, and downtown retail stores find it more convenient, for a variety of reasons, to deal with communities and their spokesmen. There are simply too many neighborhoods for downtown VIPs to comprehend. Chicago, it is estimated, contains about a hundred communities, but far more than five hundred neighborhoods.

When Edgewater eventually reappeared as a community in the late 1970s, it rode on the sturdy shoulders of its neighborhoods. Their vitality, the energy of their leaders, and the residents' concern for their own neighborhood's future (not that of the community as a whole, at first) restored Edgewater to the map of Chicago. These urban neighborhoods offered Edgewater a foundation on which to reassert itself, and, for the first time, to challenge effectively the political, economic, and social forces which were eroding neighborhoods while submerging Edgewater's identity as a community. As the neighborhoods began to define themselves, they also identified themselves with the larger community through which they could weld their individual strengths into a more effective voice.

The Lakewood-Balmoral Neighborhood

How was such a feat possible? Take the case of one such neighborhood, called Lakewood-Balmoral after the two residential streets which intersect at its center. During the middle 1970s it was described as Edgewater's "most energetic neighborhood." But Lakewood-Balmoral had been tugged in two directions since the 1960s. Because

Thirteen Neighborhoods but a Single Community

it lay strategically in the center of "Uptown" Community Area #3, the Lakewood-Balmoral neighborhood was claimed by both the Edgewater Community Council and the Uptown Chicago Commission, whose respective southern and northern boundaries then overlapped.

Originally, Lakewood-Balmoral was developed on suburban farm land as a housing subdivision before the turn of the century. The real estate broker's plan called for building attractive, one-of-a-kind, single family residences in the area's twelve square blocks. Later brick and stone-front two-flats were constructed, varying the housing style. By the 1930s the neighborhood looked physically much as it does today.

Lakewood-Balmoral aged gracefully. Some families—Swedish, German or Irish — stayed on through three generations. When their children were grown, many moved away, and families of different nationalities quickly arrived to take their place. Immediately after World War II, the neighborhood largely succeeded in shielding itself from property owners who would try to convert large, older homes into rooming houses in order to capitalize on the postwar housing crunch. Marge Britton, a second generation resident who, with her young family, now lives one block from the house where she grew up, describes Lakewood-Balmoral as she knew it:

> After the war years, life settled down. Lakewood-Balmoral was solid, stable, mostly Republican, family-oriented, and church-going. Residents were concerned with the welfare of their children and the neighborhood's institutions. On every block, in homes and two-flats, were a variety of residents, elderly couples, second generation inhabitants, new folk, owners, and some renters who became owners when they found the neighborhood suited them well enough to stay. They reflected the ethnic variety of the city and took pride in their diversity. Physically, Lakewood-Balmoral was more the prototype of a small Ohio town than an urban neighborhood in a vast metropolis. Its quiet streets, trimmed lawns, flower gardens and Victorian homes looked much like they did earlier in the century. As a compact little neighborhood it could have been about as much an anachronism as a horse and buggy, but, though it looked like 1910, its spirit was contemporary urban. And the message it conveyed was that a neighborhood resolved to do something about its future could be successful in confronting

the massive problems of present day cities. Neighborhoods such as ours were the source of the city's vitality.

When my husband, who grew up in Indiana, proposed to me in 1961, little did he realize that he was not only marrying me but also my neighborhood.

But all was not bliss in the dozen square blocks that time almost, but not quite, forgot. Around 1965, encroaching decay began to alarm residents. The neighborhood's social environment was disturbed with reports of stolen bicycles, purse snatchings and house burglaries. Signs of physical deterioration appeared in the neighborhood — an occasional vacant house or sagging porch, abandoned cars, broken fences, and dilapidated garages. Even more serious indications of trouble popped up in adjacent areas, on Winthrop and Kenmore Avenues to the east and in Uptown to the south. As residents strolled eastward to enjoy Lake Michigan or sent their children off to its beaches, they noticed that properties between their neighborhood and the lake had begun to look seedy. Apartment buildings were boarded up. Vagrants appeared on the streets which residents traveled to shop. Newspaper accounts of gang crimes in the vicinity shook up the neighborhood. From the halfway houses for patients evicted from state mental hospitals, dazed and confused persons wandered through the business districts along Broadway Avenue and intersecting commercial streets. Before long, residents were being told by friends who lived in outlying communities:

You're living in a changing community. It's no longer the urban utopia you imagined. Edgewater is teetering. Take a second look at what is happening to the Winthrop-Kenmore corridor. Even your old-timers are growing skeptical about your neighborhood's future. Your young marrieds are fleeing to the suburbs.

The conventional wisdom suggested that Lakewood-Balmoral was in the path of impending deterioration; that in a few years the neighborhood itself would be overwhelmed by disastrous change; and that the smart thing was to pack up and scoot. Mrs. Britton and her neighbors resisted. She explained:

My neighbors saw our area as an enjoyable place to live. Block parties, social gatherings, a garden walk, a musical festival, an annual winter party, and the naming of a Good Neighbor of the

Year enlivened the camaraderie. We found real friends, creating bonds of loyalty and warmth not usually associated with city living. We shared child care, car pools, exchanged information and, sometimes, resources. We treasured our neighborhood network of support.

Communal experiments of the 1960s failed, but the communal spirit of Lakewood-Balmoral thrived and became a source of pride for its residents. The birth of a baby was greeted by a parade of neighbors bringing hot dinners daily to the door of the new parents. A death was a shared tragedy. Someone was always there to talk about child-raising, aging parents, personal difficulties. Neighbors kept a watchful eye on each other's homes.

After marathon discussions over coffee cups and back fences, some residents joined a committee on community life started by St. Ita Church, the Catholic parish that embraced, within its boundaries, all of Lakewood-Balmoral. The committee soon enlisted a team of volunteers to visit the nursing homes which were proliferating just outside the neighborhood. But when committee members began discussing how St. Ita Church might safeguard Edgewater, they struck out. One member said.:

Our churches find themselves tottering somewhere between the City of God and the secular city, preaching peace, justice and social responsibility, but worrying about the stability of their own congregations and their own future.

To our idealists, our churchmen, in fact our own people, we are selling hope, a most acceptable commodity and one that's much needed in our community.

As the nursing home volunteers continued their visits, the committee's consensus was that a parish committee could have little, if any, significant impact on housing decay and deterioration.

The committee on community life voted itself out of existence; some of its members reconvened one evening and invited other neighbors, not members of the parish, to join them. Out of this and subsequent meetings in 1969 came the Lakewood-Balmoral Residents' Council. While the Council was being organized, another church in the neighborhood, the North Shore Baptist, proposed to tear down a two-story residence commanding one corner of a residential block and then pave the lot for parking. Neighbors reacted strongly and recruited sixty residents to appear before the Chicago Zoning Board of Appeals to ask that the request for a special use permit for a parking lot be denied. What happened? The pastor of the church, at first upset, then impressed by the unexpected outpouring of concern from his neighbors, withdrew the application and became a staunch backer of the Council. Several weeks later, the founding meeting of the Lakewood-Balmoral Residents Council was hosted by none other than the North Shore Baptist Church. The Council had become an ecumenical venture.

Defensive Steps

The neighborhood described by realtors as quaint and Victorian had made the leap from yesterday to tomorrow. The Council next took on the Chicago Park District, persuading it to buy an abandoned gas station and turn it into a tot lot for neighborhood youngsters. Surveillance was promised by the staff of the day care center of Unity Lutheran Church across the alley. Not long thereafter North Shore Baptist Church opened its doors daily for pre-school youngsters, most of whom lived on Winthrop and Kenmore Avenues. A neighbor struggling with alcoholism joined Alcoholics Anonymous; that encouraged several others to investigate the program. Eventually, at the request of the Council members, St. Ita Church began to host a weekly AA meeting.

Alarmed by an epidemic of auto accidents, the Council launched a successful campaign to have the city's Department of Streets and Sanitation install one stop sign at every street intersection. The traffic signs were a defensive measure against auto drivers who took a short cut through the Lakewood-Balmoral neighborhood during rush hours to by-pass traffic congestion on arterial streets closer to the lake. They were intended to discourage drivers from snaking their way through a residential neighborhood and thus endangering the lives of children and elderly.

About the same time, another incident occurred which reminded Lakewood-Balmoral residents that they were not in some Eden, sheltered from stormy urban weather. At a "fast food" drive-in located farther north in Edgewater but patronized regularly by Lakewood-Balmoral's residents, a street gang brutally beat up a customer one evening. The crime was witnessed by a housewife from Lakewood-Balmoral. When she agreed to testify in court, the gang threatened her — and her children — with violence. To show their solidarity, neighbors arranged for a bus to transport her and themselves to the trial of the two gang members arrested for assault and battery. They were convicted, and an uneasy peace settled in.

Earlier controversies had remained internal to the neighborhood. But no matter how hard it might try, Lakewood-Balmoral could not seclude itself from the outside world. Mrs. Britton explained:

> While neighborliness was the hallmark of Lakewood-Balmoral, out there to the east on the other side of Broadway, and to the south in Uptown, there was still trouble. Erecting a kingdom of twelve beautiful blocks isolated from the community around it was not the direction the Lakewood-Balmoralites would choose to take. Having acquired experience and displayed some muscle in dealing with internal issues, they became more self-confident, as the neighborhood began to attract the attention of community leaders outside.

Linking Up with Edgewater

As they demonstrated that they were self-starters and that they were potent advocates of neighborhood causes, the residents of Lakewood-Balmoral, without realizing it at the time, had begun constructing a bridge of leadership from their neighborhood to the community of Edgewater. For Edgewater was searching not only for its identity but also for a fresh supply of leaders.

As neighborhood associations such as the Lakewood-Balmoral Residents Council and others were organized, they exposed to the larger Edgewater community's view residents willing to volunteer time and talent not only on behalf of their neighborhood but also their community. One neighborhood activist, startled by what the Edgewater Community Council was doing, exclaimed:

> They're thieves! They creamed off our best people to lead Edgewater. Fortunately, we had others who had been waiting to step into their shoes.

For seven consecutive years, between 1971 and 1978, the presidency of the Edgewater Community Council was held by a resident of Lakewood-Balmoral. Through the same period of time, the neighborhood also furnished the Uptown Chicago Commission with three of its presidents. During one of these years, the presidents of both organizations lived on the same block in Lakewood-Balmoral. Two of the eight members of the "core group" which launched the Organization of the North East were graduates of the Lakewood-Balmoral Residents Council. As the 1980s arrived, Lakewood-Balmoral's reservoir of organizational veterans, skilled leaders and spunky advocates had not yet run dry.

Marilou Hedlund, former alderman of the 48th Ward, characterized the neighborhood as follows:

> Lakewood-Balmoral neighbors first got together because they wanted some "stop" signs — hardly a "power grab" of an issue. In my mind's eye, however, they were the real catalyst for the whole community of "family types" in Edgewater and Uptown. In 1971, when I took office, there were but a handful of block clubs here in various stages of dormancy. Today, just about every block has organized itself, generally on the Lakewood-Balmoral model. Their tone is low-keyed, responsive to problems when they arise, non-shrill. It works very well with any sensible politician!

Other Neighborhoods

The success of the Lakewood-Balmoral Residents Council was contagious. In 1969, the Lakewood-Balmoral Residents Council was the only active neighborhood association in all of Edgewater. Steadily, the Council's success story spurred adjacent neighborhoods to form their own associations. Lakewood-Balmoral was no longer unique; it was being replicated throughout Edgewater. Both the Edgewater Community Council and Lakewood-Balmoral sent out volunteer organizers to help other neighborhoods set up their own associations. They succeeded so well that by 1980 practically every acre of Edgewater fell under the jurisdiction of thirteen neighborhood groups, three of them in the Winthrop-Kenmore corridor. (See the neighborhood map on page 59.) Drivers passing through Edgewater could see signs affixed to light poles at key intersections announcing their entrance to each new neighborhood.

Thirteen Neighborhoods but a Single Community

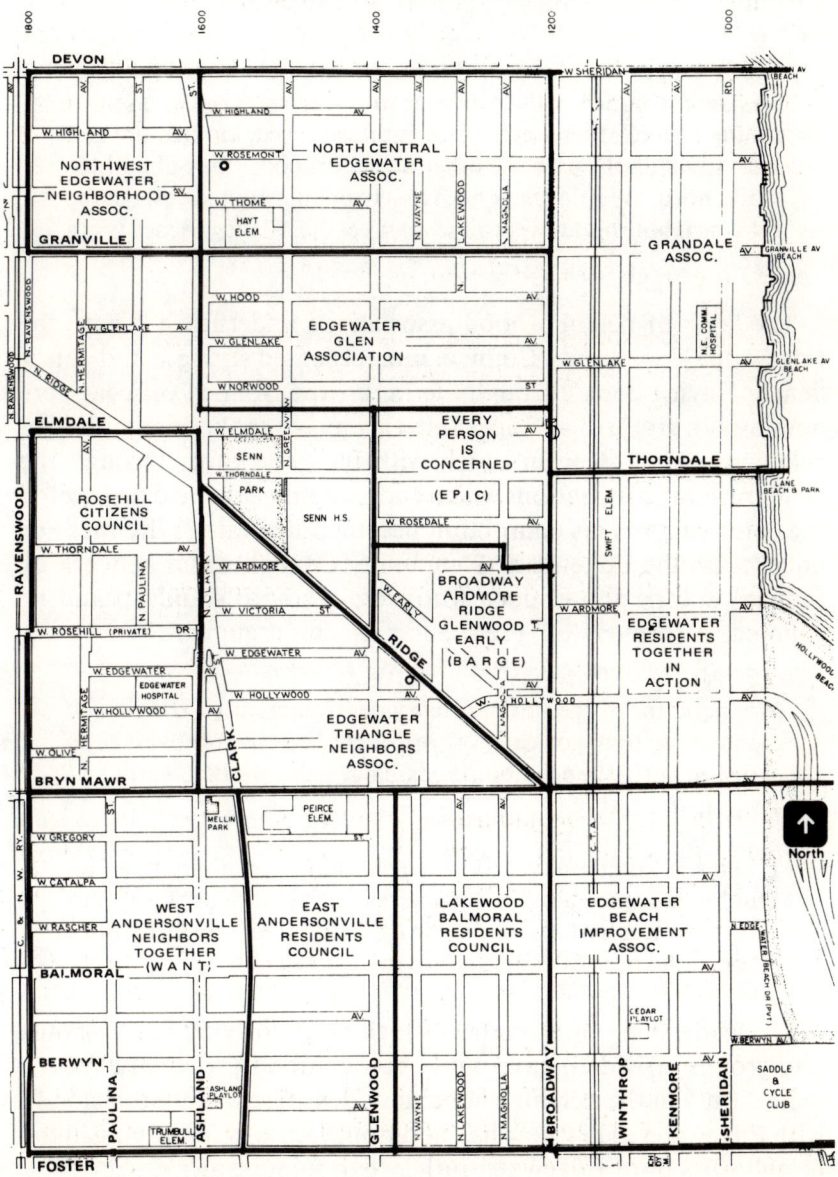

It should be emphasized that such an association did not bring a neighborhood into being but that it simply verified, self-consciously, the neighborhood's presence all along. A founder of the Lakewood-Balmoral Residents Council offered a few words of caution about the impact of the Council on the rest of Edgewater:

> Don't exaggerate the contribution of the Lakewood-Balmoral Residents Council. All we did was to pack a snowball and send it rolling through Edgewater. As it gathered speed, momentum and size, spinning through the other neighborhoods, they did all the work, not us. We may have been first to organize ourselves, but the other neighborhoods were all set to take off. All they needed was a signal.

The layer of neighborhood associations underneath it gave the Edgewater Community Council unprecedented strength and confidence. Having come through the ranks, the Council officers were not simply a group of self-appointed leaders — spokesmen without a following. They were in touch with the grass-roots through the neighborhood associations which had catapulted them to the level of the community. This connection became Edgewater's lifeline. For underneath the Edgewater Community Council was a network of families and neighborhoods who were ready to stand up and be counted. A former ECC president made this argument:

> Whenever the officers of the Edgewater Community Council take a public position, you can be sure that the issue has probably been thrashed out in the neighborhoods. That's how the ECC earns and keeps its following.
>
> I know a community group which characterizes itself as an "umbrella organization." All umbrella, I say, with only a staff to prop it up. But that's not what the ECC is. Its clout springs from a broad, solid base of people active in their neighborhoods.

The leadership opportunities, which neighborhood and community groups provided, gave public recognition to residents, rooted them firmly in the neighborhood and identified them more closely with Edgewater. They now had additional reasons for staying in the neighborhoods of Edgewater rather than running away.

Hidden in every neighborhood are women and men with a

potential for community leadership. Without a neighborhood association to give them an opportunity to display their ability, such residents would seldom be discovered — and thus not recruited — as potential leaders at the community level. Most of the officials of the Edgewater community were first schooled in neighborhood politics. In the case of the Lakewood-Balmoral Residents Council, especially in the early 1970s, the Council stood as co-equal with the Edgewater Community Council and the Uptown Chicago Commission in meetings with the Governor of Illinois and the Mayor of Chicago. When a mental health council was being organized to serve Uptown and Edgewater, members of the Lakewood-Balmoral Residents Council assumed leadership roles in the campaign.

As a mediating structure, however, the neighborhood does more than energize urban improvement by furnishing leaders. The leadership which does surface is responding to a deeper human need to deal with helplessness in the face of volatile urban change. Designed to the human scale, the neighborhood supports conservators who seek to slow down the pace of urban change so that they can grapple with it and overcome the forces that threaten the future. If neighbors are unable to control their destiny, the neighborhood inevitably self-destructs.

Settling a Boundary Dispute

A piece of unfinished business still lay on Lakewood-Balmoral's agenda: settling a friendly jurisdictional dispute between Edgewater and Uptown. For decades, the half-mile-wide section running east and west below Bryn Mawr Avenue and above Foster Avenue, two east-west streets, had been claimed by both the Uptown Chicago Commission and the Edgewater Community Council. Lakewood-Balmoral sits squarely in the middle of that strip. Before the Lakewood-Balmoral Residents Council was organized in 1969, one homeowner was heard to say:

> I live in Uptown. But my wife lives in Edgewater. And we share the same house!

In those troublesome years, it was in Uptown's self-interest to keep its northern frontier a bit vague, thus acquiring as much of Edgewater as possible to bolster Uptown's sagging image and spirits.

As long as "Uptown" was considered to be co-extensive with Community Area #3, good-natured disagreement survived. But in the 1970s, as the public perception of Edgewater's boundaries became clearer, the disputed turf came to be accepted as part of Edgewater. What crystallized public opinion was a series of neighborhood and community developments.

First, the Lakewood-Balmoral neighborhood itself began gravitating toward Edgewater. The reasons? Its housing was similar to that of other Edgewater neighborhoods west of Broadway. Furthermore, as Uptown's social problems migrated north through the corridor, Lakewood-Balmoral came to be seen as Edgewater's first zone of defense. By aligning itself with Edgewater, Lakewood-Balmoral tipped the balance in favor of Foster Avenue as the southern boundary of Edgewater and the dividing line with Uptown.

Secondly, the Uptown Chicago Commission, as it became more and more preoccupied with the severe deterioration of its commercial center, took a lackadaisical interest in the quarrel over its northern boundary. Where the Commission was lukewarm, the Edgewater Community Council was zealous and aggressive.

The ECC campaigned not only for Edgewater's identity but also for a clearer delineation of its borders. In establishing Foster Avenue as its southern limit, ECC took a popular position which would keep three neighborhoods within the confines of Edgewater: not only the Lakewood-Balmoral Residents Council and the Edgewater Beach Improvement Association, but also Andersonville to the west, which enjoyed city-wide popularity as an old Swedish settlement. Andersonville had also earned a reputation for successful retailing, thus confounding urban planners who found it hard to understand how a neighborhood commercial strip could prosper in an era of shopping centers and drive-in supermarkets.

Thirdly, unexpected support came from the Uptown 5 Guild, an Uptown community group which produced a map that located the northern border of Uptown at Foster Avenue. Having recaptured its identity in the 1970s with the help of its neighborhoods, Edgewater entered the 1980s secure that its southern border was finally in place. And Uptown showed little inclination to touch off a boundary dispute.

From Neighborhood to Community Politicians

In 1975, Lakewood-Balmoral's feisty citizenry took to the campaign trail with their own candidate for alderman to represent the 48th Ward in the Chicago City Council. Marion Kennedy Volini was the mother of five children and a former public school teacher. Her involvement in the Uptown and Edgewater communities reflected her genuine concern for the plight of mental patients who had been ruthlessly ousted from State-owned hospitals and dumped into Uptown without decent housing or adequate social and medical services. Her community-wide leadership had generated within the Lakewood-Balmoral neighborhood a desire to do something about the glut of halfway houses which were turning the Winthrop-Kenmore corridor in Uptown into a psychiatric ward, but without the services of a hospital.

Lakewood-Balmoral had spearheaded an Edgewater-Uptown community coalition to reverse the State of Illinois' policy. The proverbial straw that broke the camel's back was a State license surreptitiously granted to the owners of a large apartment hotel so that they could operate it as a 700-bed sheltered care facility for mental patients ejected from State institutions. City Hall, Lakewood-Balmoral residents concluded, was not taking seriously their complaint that public policies were hastening the degeneration of the Winthrop-Kenmore corridor. A property owner explained how he came actively to support his neighbor for alderman:

> "Downtown" told us not to worry. Only when it was too late did we realize that our City's politicians, behind our backs, had been in cahoots with their State counterparts all along. Under the humanitarian pretext of "deinstitutionalizing" the State's mental health patients, they arranged to license and subsidize a gigantic, privately-operated, profit-making institution in our community so that they could depopulate a State-owned institution located in another part of the state.
>
> Do you wonder why I jumped into aldermanic politics? The conniving had to be stopped.

Mrs. Volini lost the non-partisan election in 1975. The alderman who did win was an Uptown resident who resigned unexpectedly in the middle of his four-year term of office and migrated to the suburbs. To fill the vacancy, a special election was held in 1978. Mrs. Volini won. A year later, when the regular election took place, she ran with the triple endorsement of Democrats, Republicans and Independents—an unprecedented event in Chicago politics. Lakewood-Balmoral residents had accomplished their mission. They had persuaded the 48th ward that only a "community candidate" as alderman would represent Edgewater's authentic concerns.

5

Hard Choices: The Limits of Planning

For twenty-five years, "Uptown" had been the battlefield of recurring encounters with professional planners who arrived from the private sector as well as from City agencies. Their reports succeeded in arousing expectations for improvement, hopes often impossible to fulfill. As a result, both Uptown and Edgewater each grew more disenchanted with planners generally and with city planning in particular. This disillusionment was more noticeable and widespread in Uptown, where decades of planning seemed not to make any difference. In fact, as planners kept appearing on the Uptown scene, conditions continued to worsen — even though there was no connection between the sequence of events. The unhappy coincidence served to devalue even further the esteem in which planners were held. The following studies and reports detail "Uptown's" involvement with planning from 1957 right up to the present.

1957

The Uptown Community Area and the Southern White Immigrants: A Human Relations Study. Chicago Commission on Human Relations.

1958

Rehabilitation and Code Enforcement. Uptown Chicago Commission.

1962

Uptown: a planning report. Vols. I and II. Uptown Chicago Commission. Prepared by Jack Meltzer Associates.

1963

Uptown Rehabilitation Area, Section 134 Demonstration Project Proposal. Chicago Department of Urban Renewal.

1965

The Business Structure of the Uptown Area of Chicago. W. Ganong. MA thesis, University of Chicago.

1966

Uptown: Conservation Area Staff Report. Chicago Department of Urban Renewal.

1967

North Development Area. Chicago Department of Development and Planning.

Preliminary Staff Report: Uptown Land Use Study. Chicago Department of Urban Renewal.

Market Absorption and Land Use Study, Uptown Urban Renewal Study Area. Chicago Department of Urban Renewal. Prepared by Mid-America Appraisal and Research Corporation.

Uptown — A Pilot Rehabilitation Program. Chicago Dwellings Association. Prepared by Eugene Matanky and Associates.

Demographic Report of the Uptown Area. Chicago Tribune and *Chicago Today* newspapers, Research Division.

1968

Uptown Conservation Plan: (a) proposal for discussion purposes.

Chicago Department of Urban Renewal.

Uptown Conservation Project #1: Urban Renewal Plan. Chicago Department of Urban Renewal.

Uptown Conservation Area: The Conservation Plan. Chicago Department of Urban Renewal.

1969

Residential Facilities for Former Mental Health Patients in Uptown. The Advisory Board, Lakeview-Uptown Mental Health Center.

Conservation Plan for Project Uptown. Chicago Department of Urban Renewal.

1970

Retail Location Analysis Manual and Retailing in Low Income Areas. Chicago Economic Development Corporation. Prepared by Real Estate Research Corporation.

Impact on the Community of the Accelerated Discharge Program of Elderly Patients from Illinois State Mental Hospitals: A Statement of the Problem. Chicago Department of Human Resources.

Commercial Policies Study. Chicago Department of Development and Planning. Prepared by Mid-America Appraisal and Research Corporation.

Changing Career Patterns for the Vocationally Disadvantaged in a Polyethnic, Multicultural Model Cities Area. Jewish Vocational Services of Chicago.

To Create a New World: Plans for the Ministry of the Edgewater Presbyterian Church for the Years 1970–79. Edgewater Presbyterian Church.

Planning Framework for the Uptown People's Planning Coalition. Community Renewal Society. Prepared by Rodney Wright and Associates.

1971

Conservation Plan for the North Lakeview Section of the Uptown Model Cities Area. Vols. 1 and 2, plus Appendices. Design and Development Center, Northwestern University.

Land Use Plan: Uptown Conservation Area. Chicago Department of Urban Renewal.

Environmental Improvement Options: North Model Area. Chicago Department of Development and Planning.

Uptown Model Area Vacant Land and Abandoned Structures/ Land Use Project. Chicago Department of Development and Planning.

A Design for Community Organization Program for Uptown Center. Hull House Association, Uptown Center. Developed by Jane Addams Graduate School of Social Work, University of Illinois at Chicago Circle.

1972

Montrose/Uptown Community Development Analysis. Chicago Model Cities Program.

1973

International Plaza Feasibility Study: North Model Cities Target Area, Chicago, IL. Mayor's Committee for Economic and Cultural Development. Prepared by Larry Smith & Co.

Montrose Community Strategies. Chicago Model Cities Program.

Economic Development: Issues and Prospects. Uptown Special Projects. Prepared by Neighborhood Development Associates.

1974

Wilson Avenue Study. Uptown Chamber of Commerce. Prepared by Carl L. Gardner and Associates.

1975

Licensed Care Facilities: Some Characteristics and Community Consequences. Planning and Development Committee, Edgewater Community Council.

1976

The Psychiatric Ghetto—A Study in Non-Preparation of a Community for the Return of Former Psychiatric Patients. Marion K. Volini. (Unpublished paper presented to the annual conference of the International Association of Psycho-Social Rehabilitation Services in Chicago.)

1977

Urban Lakefront Demonstration Project: Lakefront Design Workshop. Chicago Department of Development and Planning.

Chicago Lakefront Development Benefit-Cost Analysis. Chicago Department of Development and Planning. Prepared by Lee G. Anderson and Russell F. Settle.

Hutchinson Street District. Commission on Chicago Historical and Architectural Landmarks.

1978

Peoples Development for the Heart of Uptown. Heart of Uptown Block Club Coalition.

Uptown Conservation Area. Chicago Department of Planning, City and Community Development.

Chicago's North Side Neighborhood Revitalization: Multi Faceted "Living Efficiency" Draws White, Middle Class Back to Chicago? Report of the Population and Demographics Committee, City Club of Chicago.

Evaluation of the Edgewater-Uptown Community Safety Program. Chicago Cook County Criminal Justice Commission. Prepared by Evaluation/Policy Research Associates Ltd.

Community Development Program: Neighborhood Revitalization Strategies. (Uptown NSA) Chicago Department of Planning, City and Community Development. (Working draft)

Edgewater: A diverse, unique community's recreational needs. Interim report of the Recreation Committee of the Edgewater Community Council.

A Community in Transition: The Edgewater Community in Chicago. Jane E. Ratcliffe, Loyola University of Chicago, Center for Research in Urban Government.

1979

Neighborhood Strategy Area (NSA). Preliminary Planning Statement for Uptown. Chicago Department of Human Services.

City of Chicago Application for Year V Community Development Block Grant (Uptown NSA). Chicago Department of Planning, City and Community Development and Chicago Department of Human Resources.

Preliminary Design of Proposed Urban Study. Kane, Parsons and Associates, Inc. (Working draft).

Chicago's Uptown. Elizabeth Warren, Loyola University of Chicago, Center for Research in Urban Government.

1980

An Agenda for Commercial Revitalization of Chinatown. Chicago Department of Human Services. Prepared by Neighborhood Redevelopment Assistance, Inc.

Preliminary Statement of Proposed Research on Edgewater and Uptown Communities. Edgewater Community Council. Prepared by Kathleen McCourt. (Working draft).

1981

Uptown Background for Housing Improvement. Chicago Department of Housing.

Comprehensive Plan: Argyle Redevelopment Area. Argyle Redevelopment Committee.

Uptown: Landmarks and Legends. Jacki Lyden and Chet Jakus. Organization of the North East.

Nobody was surprised in 1980 when Max Healy, executive director of the Uptown Chamber of Commerce, told a large community gathering at Harry S. Truman College that:

> Uptown has been so surveyed, so researched, so investigated, that it is now one long Ph.D. thesis.

Most planners were not neutral about Uptown. They sought viable solutions. They wanted — sometimes desperately — to improve conditions. They did succeed in stemming panic and preventing some flight. But eventually, each new batch of planners would return downtown or take jobs with some other planning body. As few visible results emerged from their activity, each new influx of planners bred deeper community dissatisfaction and cynicism toward the City's officialdom and left behind a community closer to despair. One City employee, an Uptown property owner throughout the period, reminisced:

> I felt sorry for the planners. They were babes in the Uptown wilderness. They tiptoed into our community to solve *our* problems, not knowing the first thing about the reasons why Uptown was in

trouble, why the commercial center was in bad shape, why multi-family housing was being abandoned or torched. However, that didn't stop them from coming up with proposals and answers. I have a bushel of their reports, each telling us how things were going to get better.

They were inexperienced in dealing with local businessmen and developers; they didn't know the first thing about encouraging self-help, rehabilitation, reinvestment or marketing. Their inflexibility discouraged a working partnership with community groups and institutions who searched for a vehicle through which their voices could be heard.

The planners saw themselves as regulating or coordinating private development but were seldom savvy enough to stimulate it. So enchanted were they with the notion that downtown could deliver whatever was promised, they disregarded what our own neighborhoods could do to help families help themselves.

We appealed to the City's Commissioner of Planning to halt the avalanche of former mental patients and drug addicts, ex-alcoholics, public aid recipients and disruptive multi-problem families that were descending upon Uptown as a result of calculated City and State policy. Instead of coming to our aid, the City's chief planner fed us doubletalk.

After we got around to translating his message, we realized that he had written off Uptown as a piece of dead real estate and that he was willing to let Uptown's corridor become one gigantic poorhouse.

Despite the failings of the planning profession in "Uptown" over the last twenty years, the overall reaction to planners today, among residents of the Winthrop-Kenmore corridor, is far more realistic. A housing lawyer observed that:

There is now a much healthier, more tolerant attitude towards planning among Uptown's leadership. They better understand its limitations, no longer expect planners to reverse urban decline. They see better the special responsibility of the Planning Department to express the City's position while incorporating somehow

Hard Choices: the Limits of Planning

the community's point of view. Nobody any longer expects planners to produce a magic wand which will make our problems vanish. The new attitude is good for them — and for us too.

Edgewater's situation is different. As it became organized, won recognition downtown and began making political waves, the City Hall politicians started to respond, offering to help. How could they? That's the question for which Edgewater needs an answer. It's one thing to deal effectively with initiatives from the planning establishment, but when it comes to looking to the community for suggestions, that puts the responsibility back in Edgewater.

Charles P. Livermore, a deputy commissioner of the City's Department of Planning in the 1970s, convinced many City department heads to take a searching look at the importance of the community and its institutions to the formulation of City policy and to the revitalization of Chicago. Livermore underscored the danger when a community expects too much of urban planners:

> What is the importance of planners turning their attention to neighborhoods? They can influence the flow of resources to neighborhoods. They can prevent increasing housing densities. They can stop objectionable land uses. They can modify streets, "cul-de-sac" them, bend them, "parkway" them. They can locate community institutions. They can map and name neighborhoods. They can maintain inventories of neighborhood resources. They can report and maintain histories of neighborhoods. They can monitor business prosperity and investment trends in neighborhoods. They can help appoint advisory groups, create new agencies, establish boundaries for service districts. They can make noises that attract private investment. They can identify models of appropriate institutional responses to community problems.
>
> These are things planners can do; they are also things almost anyone can do. Whose job is it to see that they do in fact get done? In Edgewater and Uptown the communities have organized themselves to get this job done.
>
> Planners often see themselves as the theologians of public policy. I can understand the significance of their rhetoric. But there are far better explanations for the revival of the neighborhoods in the 1970s.

The Planner's Dilemma

Another roadblock to reviving a community in trouble arises from the planner's slowness to appreciate how some goals cancel out others, no matter how eloquent their protagonists may be. Hence accusations of bad faith or self-interest surface to thwart reasonable discussion of conflicting community objectives. And thus hard choices are often postponed. Three examples from the Winthrop-Kenmore corridor help illuminate the dilemma:

● At a block club meeting, a resident reported that the owner of a six-apartment building had obtained a rehabilitation loan. Two outbursts simultaneously arose from the audience of owners and renters — one of joy, the other of dismay. For property owners, the bank loan foreshadowed additional investment for improvement and the resurgence of their block; it hinted that depressed property values would finally move upward. For tenants it meant higher monthly rents and the likelihood that some would have to move. In the discussion that followed, a Puerto Rican mechanic who had recently bought a modest two-flat argued defensively:

> I'm not proud of my building now. It needs lots of repair, inside and out. I can hardly pay the mortgage. If I start making improvements, who is going to pay for them? My tenants will have to help me by paying a higher rent. They will benefit too. There's no other way. I want my building to be the nicest one on the block. I want the best for my wife and kids.

● Long-time residents feared racial change far less than they did the new underclass, whether it was black, white, brown, yellow or red. They preferred racial integration to an economic mix which resulted from the multiplication of single-parent families receiving public aid or of drifters who had never held a steady job. A black school teacher gave her version of the dominant viewpoint:

> I want to live in a racially integrated community. Edgewater's a good place for my growing children. Most blacks and whites genuinely want the same things. But some blacks don't give a damn; they prefer resegregation and hope the whites will be scared away. I'm against drunkards, prostitutes and con artists, without regard to race, color or nationality. They're the ones who threaten

Hard Choices: the Limits of Planning

me — and my white neighbors. Yet when we speak out together against them, some white do-gooder who lives elsewhere promptly shows up to excuse their exotic behavior and to charge us with being cruel and insensitive.

● A new owner was nonplussed to discover the hazards of ownership in the Winthrop-Kenmore corridor.

I bought an apartment building. Originally, it had six apartments, now converted to twelve. It was in bad shape — inside and out. The back porch was unsafe, the stairs dangerous to climb. The mailbox locks were broken. No light fixtures had been changed in years. The hallways and plumbing needed repair. But it was a solidly-built building located in a block that looked like it was up and coming. Architecturally, the building was attractive, if you could see past the poor maintenance and tuckpointing. In my mind's eye, I could see its rehabilitation as a community improvement.

But I discovered that physical upgrading was a breeze compared to my confrontation with the occupants. On the first floor, I found three prostitutes and a pimp. (I was told there were actually six, but I never found out.) On the third floor lived an auto thief who practiced his profession on the night shift. Alcoholics and drug addicts peopled the other apartments. On the second floor the guys who twice had started fires while smoking in bed were still there. Their apartment was a pigsty. When I tried to get some of the residents to shape up or ship out, I was told that they would burn the building down; they threatened me with plunder and personal assault. I had never realized till then that collecting rent could be a hazardous occupation. To my delight, some of the lower-income families became my best tenants; they were the building's anchors as I widened my search for other good tenants.

Most planners are comfortable with urban strategies that contend with questions of land use, beautification, transportation, landscaping, and brick-and-mortar projects. They seek to improve the *place* which they have been assigned to plan. However, they do not always have the talents or training to confront problems associated with *person* and *family*: alcoholism, juvenile delinquency, child abuse, fatherless families, language and educational handicaps, unemployability, or chronic illness. Subconsciously, planners relegate such ills to social workers, educators, clergy, counsellors and the like.

When planners see a neighborhood solely as several blocks of buildings and not also as a network of families, it becomes an enigma to them, an obstacle which they somehow must overcome if residents are to be helped. But real solutions to inner city problems, such as those that face the Winthrop-Kenmore corridor, depend on changes in both place *and* person. Nowhere is this more evident than in the confusion about what meaning to attach to a slum. Is it simply a piece of real estate, a dilapidated building, a deteriorating strip of houses? Or is it primarily a way of life for a certain class of poor people, a social environment in which nobody cares?

In his book *The Other America*, Michael Harrington reaches the heart of the matter:

> A slum is not merely an area of decrepit buildings. It is a social fact. There are neighborhoods in which housing is run-down, yet the people do not exhibit the hopelessness of the other Americans. Usually, these places have a vital community life around a national culture or religion. In New York City, Chinatown is an obvious example. Where the slum becomes truly pernicious is when it becomes the environment of the culture of poverty, a spiritual and personal reality for its inhabitants as well as an area of dilapidation. This is when the slum becomes the breeding ground of crime, of vice, the creator of people who are lost to themselves and to society.

A high school counsellor described the planning paradox:

> I know dozens of adults who were surprised to learn that they had been born and raised in a slum. Years afterwards, they were informed that their house and block had been designated as a slum or blighted area because of physical appearances and conditions. The name-calling planner with a middle-class background was never able to comprehend what was happening inside those buildings or to recognize that the place, for ninety percent of the families, was a distinct improvement over their previous housing.

The heavy concentration of urban poverty and despair—whether in a gargantuan public housing project or in a residential community which has been abandoned by merchants, banks, lawyers, doctors, and religious institutions—continues as the most serious unsolved problem on the urban agenda for the 1980s.

Hard Choices: the Limits of Planning

Trying to treat person *and* place simultaneously produces no magic formula that guarantees instant success. The landlord of a sixteen-apartment building in the Winthrop-Kenmore corridor offered his version of the dilemma facing planners:

> You can really upgrade a residential block: tear down the dangerous structures, rehabilitate fine, old buildings and build new housing. But what about the problem families living there? Do you simply transport them en masse to another large building on the next block?
>
> One well-founded criticism of urban renewal was that it successfully relocated the target area's social problems to the adjoining neighborhood which would then be ready for more urban renewal.

The head of a tenants council in a recently-built, but already deteriorating, high-rise subsidized by the Department of Housing and Urban Development supplied an additional perspective:

> Sure we have squatters and non-rent payers. Some may even be dope addicts. But all of them have rights too. Why should they be evicted or dispersed? We're going to resist every move to dump our no-income families into the street.
>
> We want the building manager to upgrade our building, fix the plumbing, clean the halls, wash the outside windows, make sure that the elevators run, remove the litter from the parkway, plant grass, shrubs and trees, and stop hassling our kids. Is that asking too much?

The pastor of a church serving residents of the Winthrop-Kenmore corridor rounded out the discussion:

> The price to pay for not revitalizing the corridor is too high. It means keeping the poor poor; perpetuating neighborhoods which are peopled by families who all belong to a single class, families overwhelmed by personal problems ranging from bankruptcy to unemployment; and having to justify unconscionable governmental practices which cram poverty, dependency, delinquency and prostitution into the same neighborhood. A neighborhood like this doesn't realize it's been hit by a government-produced tornado. Such a neighborhood seldom protests what is being done to it.

How can I remain silent in the face of such injustice? In their present environment, many of my parishioners have little hope for a better life here on earth.

As Edgewater in the early 1970s began confronting the urban decay moving into its community via the Winthrop-Kenmore corridor, the planning climate had changed. City planners and spenders had become more modest about their promises. Administrators of federal programs were re-assessing the premises behind programs which had failed to revive "Uptown" in previous decades. Citizens were now better prepared and organized to take their own initiatives to retard further deterioration of the corridor. Combining their political strength and using their City Hall connections, Edgewater's citizenry discovered that it was not so difficult to halt or delay some urban project which they saw as harming their community. What was frustrating was their inability to stimulate residential rehabilitation and to attract owners who would improve their properties. Commercial streets presented an even greater obstacle, since merchants displayed little or no enthusiasm for making their stores and shops more attractive, keeping their streets and sidewalks rubbish-free, or taking an active part in community revitalization. Important also was the discouraging fact that many of the shopkeepers lived outside the community. Recognizing that many of the traditional approaches would be inadequate to reverse the decline, Edgewater's neighborhood leaders were ready to take new steps toward community revitalization.

6

Urban Strategies That Work

As a community menaced in the 1970s the way Uptown had been two decades previously, Edgewater stood better prepared to wrestle with similar threats to its vitality as an urban community. Edgewater's leaders had learned their lessons from Uptown's earlier experience with the debilitating impact of crowded poverty, with the bewilderment of owners of vacant, multi-apartment buildings, and with a government bureaucracy so preoccupied with cost-cutting that the local community's well-being was disregarded.

In both communities the local leadership, now re-invigorated, had made use of traditional approaches to urban revitalization:

— stricter observance of building, zoning and fire codes;
— elimination of street corner prostitution;
— addition of "beat" policemen to prevent crime;
— organizing block clubs and neighborhood associations;
— activating local chambers of commerce and business groups;
— publicizing commitments by lending institutions to invest money in local rehabilitation projects;
— multiplication of block parties and neighborhood celebrations;
— beautification and clean-up campaigns;
— ensuring attentive social services;
— monitoring city departments to assure regular garbage pick-up,

- street cleaning and tree planting;
- more park space and supervised recreation for youngsters;
- modernization of elevated train stations;
- downzoning to dilute urban densities;
- demolition of dangerous and dilapidated buildings;
- reduction of arson by increasing tenant alertness and better police work;
- new patterns of street traffic to safeguard pedestrians and to speed up the movement of autos; and
- provision of more off-street parking in commercial areas.

Even when diligently applied in Edgewater and Uptown, such standard approaches produced disappointing results, disproportionately small outcomes for the effort invested. Hence the citizenry living in or next to the Winthrop-Kenmore corridor undertook to borrow or devise, and then to test in the 1970s, a score or more of newer urban approaches that curbed blight, spurred neighborhood improvement, and renewed homeowner faith in the community's future. Without proposing them as urban panaceas, a dozen such community initiatives are worth singling out as effective approaches to urban revitalization.

#1. Use the voters' broom to sweep clean a political organization which profits from urban misery.

For all practical purposes, the lakefront communities on the north side of Chicago sustain three political parties: regular Democrats who ordinarily represent the city's political establishment; Republicans who are generally demoralized even though they enjoy greater strength here than in other Chicago wards; and Independents who attract disillusioned Democrats, straying Republicans and those disbelievers in the political party process who tend to follow the political cues of a daily newspaper. Though the Democrats are the majority party, an alliance of Republicans, Independents and A.W.O.L Democrats can achieve political reform by electing "community candidates" who then hold office, though sometimes only for one term.

In Uptown and Edgewater the Democratic political establishment endured because it could commandeer, on election day, a bloc of voters who lived in halfway houses, nursing homes, sheltered care facilities, flophouses, boarding and rooming houses which cater to the elderly poor, or in residential hotels. These "hotels" were described by Lesley Sussman, a reporter for the *Rogers Park-Edgewater News* as:

> ...fancy names for flophouses with the only real difference that instead of paying a couple of bucks a night for a bed, the men and women who live in these dives pay rents of $125 per month or more.
>
> These "roach hotels," as they're known along the streets of Uptown and Edgewater, are home to down-and-out alcoholics who would otherwise be sleeping in the streets.
>
> Their rent is paid from monthly public aid or Social Security checks, and for the price they get one room, a sink, a bathroom and a menagerie of roaches, mice and rats....
>
> The Illinois Department of Public Aid certainly doesn't care. Once a month this agency will send a case worker to these residential hotels for a cursory visit...to make certain that the checks it mails each month are being sent to people who are still alive. And the Social Security Administration doesn't give a damn either. This agency doesn't even bother to send anyone around, because, after all, that's not its job.

Sussman could also have said that in some residential hotels the roomers never even see their monthly check. The manager takes it in the morning mail and cashes it, deducts the rent and other sundries, and doles out the remainder as the roomer demands it. Some Uptown hotel managers were once sent to jail for cashing the public aid checks of men and women who had been dead for months. A precinct captain, formerly associated with the corrupt (and corrupting) 48th Ward Regular Democratic Organization, which covers nearly two-thirds of Edgewater and a good part of Uptown, revealed how this system works:

> In the 1960s the organization could count on several thousand such votes on election day. That number is now down to over a thousand. In a close election that's still the margin of victory. When that chain which links destitution, prostitution, skid row and the mentally ill to political triumph is broken, Uptown and

Edgewater will enjoy more honest politics.

In 1981 the great majority of the 48th Ward's Democratic precinct captains don't even live in the ward; many live in the suburbs as political commuters. They could care less about our community. When election day is in sight, they come out of their suburban woodwork to re-install their system for shuttling their voters, illegally or otherwise, to the polling place with instructions on how to vote.

In their own way, the Republicans helped me carry my precinct. They were scarce, and those that were around were scared to serve as election day juges in my kind of precinct. So on election day we simply gave the two slots assigned to the GOP to our own Democrats who pretended to be Republicans from 6 a.m. to 6 p.m.

It's a hellish circle of vice and poverty. I know. I was part of it. One of my rooming houses furnished each voter a dirty bed in a dingy room. A day labor agency supplied temporary labor and a check at the end of the work day. The nearby bar cashed the check that same evening and catered to alcoholic needs while streetwalkers hung around to pick up any remaining change. On election day my victory margin was twenty-to-one. If it was a bad day, my winning ratio slipped to ten-to-one.

To make sure this voting majority was around on election day, the politicians higher up had to protect the rooming house, the tavern and the day labor agency from being cited for violating the city's health, safety, fire or building code. Were the code to be observed, these places couldn't afford to stay open. They would be shut and eventually torn down, drastically depleting the organization's reserve of manipulated voters.

As the number of rooming houses and residential hotels decreased, the power base of the 48th Ward's political organization began to shift as well, forcing it to be more responsive to another class of voters: homeowners, condominium buyers, family renters and businessmen.

#2. Give the exploiting day labor agencies tougher competition so that the worst ones move away or go out of business.

Uptown's skid row along Broadway and Wilson Avenues, a syndrome of shady taverns, flophouses and recruiters of temporary labor, is slowly disappearing. Many of the disreputable bars and flophouses have been razed. Most of Uptown's neighborhoods have successfully resisted further encroachment from day labor agencies. Community pressure for stricter observance of laws, building, fire and zoning codes has begun to pay off.

Key to the changeover was organizing in 1970 a not-for-profit day labor office called Just Jobs, which sought to curb the human exploitation of industrial day laborers. A second not-for-profit agency, Amos, opened its doors in the late 1970s. Both were started with financial aid from the Campaign for Human Development, the self-help anti-poverty agency of the Catholic bishops of the United States. To improve the day laborers' working conditions, Just Jobs paid them a higher wage, tried to steer them away from the arms of bartenders at the day's end, and officially notified companies, contrary to the established practice of temporary labor offices, that no fee would be charged if an assigned worker was offered permanent employment. Not only did such a sales approach benefit the marginal workers who hired themselves out as day laborers, but it also appealed to employers for reasons of good business and social conscience. In the 1970s the tough competition from decent employers of day labor, such as Just Jobs, helped Uptown rid the area of many of its worst exploiters of temporary labor.

#3. Mobilize the precinct electorate to rid the neighborhood of undesirable liquor stores and other trouble spots.

As urban blight seeps into a neighborhood, often the first unwelcome sign is a disorderly tavern or package liquor store which sells to minors or entices boozy patrons who then spill onto the sidewalk. Police often have to be summoned to break up a brawl or to prevent constant annoyance to women passing by. The issue is not the corner bar or the local hangout but its removal as a neighborhood hazard, a magnet for crime, soliciting, narcotics, or violence. To put an end to such hooliganism, on election day citizens have the right to vote a political precinct "dry", ending the sale of liquor within its boundaries. Or community representatives can call for a public hearing to protest the city's renewal of an obnoxious tavern's liquor license. On occasion, both stratagems have been used successfully in Uptown and Edgewater. Even the *threat* of precinct balloting has been effective in persuading many a tavern owner to clean up his joint. To avoid a vote that might put his bar out of business, he takes the initiative to end the disorderly conduct to which his neighbors have been objecting. In most urban areas voters are understandably reluctant to prohibit the selling of alcoholic beverages. Only a public nuisance would provoke them enough to vote a "wet" precinct "dry". In Chicago, all precincts are, as a matter of course, "wet" until the constituents decide otherwise. On any given election day in Chicago, such wet-or-dry contests invariably take place in the precincts of neighborhoods fighting to come back.

Similarly, an "adult" bookstore, or a "porno parlor" as it is popularly known, is clearly perceived by parents as a menace to their families. It signals to a neighborhood that it is under siege and that it had better counterattack. Mrs. Britton, a former president of the Lakewood-Balmoral Residents Council, described how, after several unsuccessful attempts to persuade the building owner, one such bookstore finally departed:

> Children from two different schools had to pass this store each morning and afternoon. The store was in a large building which had several shops on the first floor and residences on the second. Because of the age of the building, we suspected that the electrical wiring was faulty and dangerous, so we asked the City's building department to come out and inspect the entire building. We tracked down the building owner (it wasn't easy) and found that he lived in a plush high-rise on Lake Shore Drive, miles away from the bookstore. One Saturday morning, a hundred neighbors with their school-age children dressed up in their Sunday best, got into their autos, and went to picket his high-rise. We mimeographed and distributed leaflets explaining why we were there. As we exercised our constitutional right of free speech, we even picked up words of encouragement; the residents there said they wouldn't want one of those places in their building either. A few weeks later the "dirty" bookstore was gone, and in its place appeared—a dry cleaning shop.

#4. Confront head-on the community's perception of dangerous streets as well as the crime rate itself.

Before World War II, "safe streets" meant: Are our streets safe for roller skating, hopscotch, baseball, bicycles and jumping rope— as more cars raced faster down them? Today any question about

Urban Strategies That Work

"safe streets" carries more ominous significance: Will I be mugged or robbed? Will someone snatch my purse? Are the children safe from molestation? Is it too risky to walk to church after dark? Neighborhoods wither away without that pedestrian contact which is promoted by homeowners venturing outside to mow and water their lawns or by children walking to school or playground. The mother of four young girls explained:

> I know for a fact that last year crime went down in my neighborhood. But in talking to my neighbors, I discovered that their perception of crime had gone up.
>
> My neighbors, like most Americans, were concerned about street crime, home burglaries and drug peddlers. Whatever the local crime rate might be, their growing fears governed their unwillingness to use streets, sidewalks, and city parks. As the pedestrian forsakes city streets, they inevitably become more dangerous. A self-fulfilling prophecy works again.

In 1980 a cartoonist captured for *Modern Maturity* magazine the national preoccupation with crime in the cities:

To deflate fears and to encourage pedestrian mobility, the Edgewater Community Council sponsored several "walks" and "tours" along Winthrop and Kenmore Avenues for condominium owners in the Sheridan Road high-rises. Most of the participants had previously been afraid to walk these streets; some expressed surprise at seeing beautiful homes and excellent architecture. The tour was planned to show the strollers the best and worst to be found in the corridor. The Council's purpose was to use the Sheridan Road "grapevine" for increased communication, for sifting fact from fiction, for mobilizing untapped resources, for encouraging Sheridan Road condominium owners to identify with the Edgewater community and for bringing unspoken fears out into the open. High-rise dwellers, surveys reveal, tend to be more skittish than those who live on the street level.

Two other Council programs were directed to quieting irrational fears about street crime as much as they were to crime prevention. The first of these was Operation WhistleSTOP, whose national headquarters are in the Council's office. Mary Garrity, whose team of WhistleSTOP volunteers had sold 300,000 whistles nationwide by 1981, explained their importance:

> It is a community signal system for trouble on the streets or for any emergency when police response is needed. WhistleSTOP gives a community a way to reclaim its own streets. Not a reckless one, but a sense that when citizens are in trouble, they can count on each other for assistance.
>
> Residents blow their whistles to signal trouble—and when they hear the signal they know that a neighbor is in distress. Then they call the police and blow their own whistle to attract additional attention. The distinctive sound of the whistle ties the isolated pedestrian to his neighbors and through them to the police. It is the only safe, non-violent weapon a pedestrian can carry on his person at all times. The whistle has a breakaway chain; a criminal cannot use it to hurt its wearer.
>
> As a community safety program, WhistleSTOP fights crime on the streets, improves police-community relations and fosters a new sense of community. Good neighbors make safer communities.

Is it any surprise that the most popular piece of "costume jewelry" in Edgewater is a shiny whistle hanging from a chain around a woman's neck or on a man's key ring?

The Council's other crime prevention program, co-sponsored with the Uptown Chicago Commission, is a radio patrol staffed by two dozen volunteers. They drive the streets of Edgewater and Uptown during the late evening and early morning hours on weekends, serving as extra eyes and ears for the police and fire departments. The volunteers carry portable radios to keep in touch with each other and with a base station which reports suspicious events to the police. What good does the radio patrol do? A volunteer answers:

> Security on our streets is ninety percent mental. The other ten percent is being a little more careful at night.

#5. Establish an escort service to provide moral support to witnesses who appear in court, to prevent their being intimidated by street gangs or bamboozled by shyster lawyers.

A sure sign that neighborhood deterioration has started is the unwillingness of residents to complain about unlawful activity or to come to the rescue of someone in trouble. This reluctance may stem from the fear of retaliation by a gang or from the lack of any sense of loyalty to one's neighbors. No neighborhood can last long when its social climate is uncaring, irresponsible or isolationist. Frightened residents and transiency are tragic symptoms of a dying neighborhood.

Can neighbors help ensure that, when the law is clearly on their side, wrongs will be righted and justice done? Yes, when witnesses come forward to testify or when complaints are filed and then followed up doggedly. It is now the custom in many of Edgewater's neighborhoods for neighbors to rally behind a complainant and to accompany a witness to court. A bus may be chartered or a car pool organized to transport the witness and the concerned neighbors to the courthouse.

Edgewater's spontaneous escort service became a regular practice after a street gang, called the TJOs, terrorized a section of Edgewater where Letty and Bill Cooper lived with their ten children. Cooper was a carpenter by trade, and Mrs. Cooper worked part-time as a nurse. One July evening he was in front of his house talking to a neighbor. A car roared up the one-way street the wrong way. Cooper shouted: "It's a one-way." The driver, a leader of the TJOs, pulled into the alley and began yelling obscenities. Cooper went over to tell him that such language with children around was offensive. Cooper's wife told what happened next:

He slugged Bill, knocked him down, then set him back up and kicked him in the face with his boot. Bill was in the hospital three days while doctors re-attached his eyelid and tried to stop the hemorrhaging behind the eye. Bill signed a complaint. So did others who had been victimized by the same gang. One was a woman who had been hit on the head with a rock. Some had been robbed. Whenever the gang learned who was filing complaints, they would promptly threaten the plaintiffs with bodily harm. Elderly people are easily intimidated by loud, foul language and lewd gestures.

Never having been to a court before in my life, I really thought they were all going to be Perry Masons. It was quite a revelation. When we got there, the judge would order a continuance. Then we were never sure who the state's attorney would be—they kept changing—and none of them realized how the community was being terrorized. We had to tell our story over and over. It was ridiculous. Nobody understands the criminal justice system. But the criminals and their lawyers do. We were really put at a great disadvantage.

Sixty people from the neighborhood came to court to lend us support. Was that great!

For every court appearance (the total eventually came to fifty!) transportation had to be arranged, baby-sitters found. Forty-two complaints were ultimately filed against the gang and its members. Thirty-nine convictions resulted. Mr. Cooper's assailant was convicted on a charge of aggravated battery. The turnout of neighbors so impressed the judge that he resisted granting further continuances. The gang's lawyer had hoped to wear down the complainants and witnesses, knowing that some had to take a day off from work to appear in court.

The escort service applies to the housing court as well. When a landlord is cited for multiple violations of the building and fire codes, neighbors who regard the building as a community eyesore do not sit back and wait to see what the judge will do. They show up in court. One court watcher explained:

When someone goes to court, it's not just a personal matter; it's a community problem. You never let someone go alone. Your neighbors are there—silent witnesses—to show that we all care.

Moral support becomes very important when threats are made. In housing court, building code violations are routine stuff to the judge. But when a dozen neighbors show up, the judge takes a special interest in the case. We found that a bus load of neighbors gets better results.

In a lively neighborhood the escort service works in still other ways. A parent from Edgewater's Lakewood-Balmoral neighborhood recounted his experience:

> Our relatives call us screwballs because we want to live in the city and raise our children here and not in some suburb. Neighboring is what we're good at.
>
> In the next block a widow with teen-age boys and girls kept her home open for all the teen-agers living on the street. She became the block's foster mother. When her husband died, she went to college to get a degree so that she could get a teaching job. On the day of graduation, grateful neighbors decided to celebrate the event with her. They hired a limousine and a liveried chauffeur to drive her back from the commencement exercises. A block party followed, and she was the celebrity.

#6. Rid the community of abandoned autos which litter streets and vacant lots, by cutting through the legal and bureaucratic red tape.

Abandoned autos are the scourge of a community threatened with blight. Once they start to appear on streets, alleys or vacant lots, other frustrated car owners swarm nearby, turning the community into a junkyard. Stolen cars are easily left in the area and stripped of their parts by night. Castoff vehicles become dangerous, attractive nuisances for children who are tempted to break windows and headlights or to set fires. Where abandoned autos are everywhere in sight, families are unlikely to rent apartments or buy a home, particularly if they own a new auto themselves.

City and state legislation intended to control auto theft and safeguard property rights specifies an elaborate set of procedures before any vehicle can be towed away. In the late 1960s and early 1970s these regulations supplied city departments with endless excuses for not removing hundreds of motored derelicts which could be seen on any given day, but especially after a harsh and snowy winter. By forcing the government to admit that many of the regulations were legal nonsense and should be discarded, Uptown and Edgewater managed to bring automobile abandonment under reasonable control.

It was simply a matter of asking the right questions. Is it a piece of junk or an automobile? If it has no motor, no headlight, no battery, no wheels, if its upholstery is spilling out and burned, is it bulk trash —to be treated like any other large piece of junk? An auto which is abandoned can usually be recognized as a ruin. Why dignify the sad collage of metal and plastic by calling it an automobile?

Once this understanding became widespread among judges, policemen, city officials and tow truck operators, the entire removal process was speeded up by months. Nowadays, thanks to the vigilance of residents who report such abandoned "autos" promptly to the alderman's office, the clunkers are carted away with dispatch. The unrelenting pressure from communities like Edgewater and Uptown finally convinced city officials to redefine their notion of an "abandoned vehicle."

#7. Obtain from public officials a moratorium on any further licensing of sheltered care facilities in order to allow the community time to recuperate from the earlier inundation and spare it further hardship.

The Winthrop-Kenmore corridor easily contains a greater concentration of halfway houses, nursing homes, and other sheltered care facilities than any other area of the city. The corridor has aptly been described as the "world's largest psychiatric ghetto." The hapless and helpless occupants of its private properties have been abused and exploited by doctors, lawyers, landlords, judges, elected officials, planning commissioners, the Illinois Department of Mental Health, the Cook County Department of Public Aid, the Chicago Board of Health and countless others. Since the 1960s, sheltered care facilities strewn through the corridor have been the subject of repeated exposés by the daily newspapers, investigations by the Better Government Association, and public hearings of the U.S. Senate, House of Representatives, Illinois State Senate, Illinois House of Representatives and Chicago City Council. A real estate broker summed up the situation:

How do you cope with an avalanche? That's what was heading towards Edgewater up the corridor, and that's what had demolished the center of Uptown.

Financial wizards in the state bureaucracy, with the help of naive social workers, concocted noble-sounding rationalizations for emptying out the state's mental health institutions. But they were really out to cut costs. They were willing to ship out all institutionalized patients without regard to the consequences—for the patients or for the community to which they were sent.

Dr. Jack Weinberg, now director of the Illinois Mental Health Institutes, said:

> As Illinois' first psychiatrist-in-chief for extramural care, I inaugurated a program of foster home placement of the mentally ill into the community. But that was done on a case by case basis and not by mass production.... Communities have to be prepared to accept the emotionally ill and provide for their proper integration into the community, something we have not done in the "Uptown" area.

The following summary of the situation nationally, by Professor Arthur J. Naparstek of the University of Southern California, accurately describes what also devastated Uptown:

> Deinstitutionalization, an ostensibly humane treatment program, has degenerated into a tragic crisis....
>
> Planners, without real consultation, assumed that strong communities would accept the chronically ill. When few welcomed large numbers of these troubled people, patients were steered to transitional neighborhoods that would not put up a fuss, but the strong community-support factor essential for successful aftercare was absent.
>
> The result was that city streets became wards of mental hospitals, and it was out of the snakepits and into the gutter for victims of the deinstitutionalization policy.

Finally, in the early 1970s, a coalition of community organizations and churches on Chicago's north side extracted a public committment from state and city officials that no additional licenses to operate sheltered care facilities would be issued in the Winthrop-Kenmore corridor or its adjoining blocks. One Edgewater resident later testified that:

> It has been amply demonstrated that our community accepted far more than its fair share of people whom society had an obligation to assist. The time finally has come for our community to stand up and declare, "We have been socially and morally responsible. We have taken more than our fair share. But enough is enough."
>
> We will not stand idly by and acquiesce in meandering and misguided public policies which undermine our progress. The process of decay which our community has faced has been abetted by government at many levels.

In 1981 the moratorium still exists, policed by community leaders. The 1970s gave the Edgewater and Uptown communities breathing time—the opportunity to wrestle with existing social crises without having to worry about further floods of chronically ill citizens brutalized by the State policy.

#8. Encourage local institutions not to flee or to shut down but to adapt to new populations and their kaleidoscope of lifestyles.

In Uptown and Edgewater, churches and social centers have been anchors for their communities, providing stability, continuity of leadership, identity, and support. Before decline set in, these institutions had made a committment to stay and serve newcomers. Not suffering from institutional rheumatism, churches such as Bethany Lutheran, North Shore Baptist, and Unity Lutheran opened day care centers and pre-school programs. These and other houses of worship began conducting Sunday services in Korean, Japanese, Spanish, Filipino and other languages and welcomed arrivals from Asia, South America and Africa. Indians from U.S. reservations were served by St. Augustine's Center and the American Indian Center. Neighborhood centers like Hull House, Robert R. McCormick Boys Club and Christopher House revamped their recreational and counselling programs to adapt to the different cultures and increased their hours of availability during evenings and weekends.

St. Thomas of Canterbury Church is situated in the heart of

Uptown. What happens there reflects the ways an indigenous institution can accommodate its ministry to an area undergoing urban deterioration. Twice a week, the parish's soup kitchen opens up in the evening to serve rice and beans. Prayer meetings are held in nursing homes. The parish, according to the pastor, contains twenty-seven such institutions and nearly 1,000 bed-ridden parishioners, many of them senior citizens. Down the street from the church is the St. Francis house of hospitality. In a Chicago version of the Canterbury Tales, youthful members of the Jesuit Volunteer Corps and other young people journey here to live nearby and serve the needy. St. Thomas Church was described by Frances Sloan in the national magazine, *U.S. Catholic,* as "the parish that speaks five languages":

> A church which once saw ushers dressed in tuxedos and limousine-driven parishioners, St. Thomas now boasts a mural which wraps around its basement hall and depicts the fires, drug rings, rent-gouging landlords, and wrecking crews which undermine Uptown today.
>
> Hard-core misfits, from the physically deformed who have been shuttled from state institutions into one of the many halfway houses and nursing homes that dot the five-block square parish, to the Knights of the Road who have been forced out of Chicago's old skid row by urban renewal crews, are interspersed with immigrants who came to Chicago to find a job. The handicapped will stay in the nursing homes, unless the state legislates more aid for a different clientele such as the mentally ill or the elderly, but many of the immigrants will move on to a more homogenous neighborhood matching their ethnic heritage.
>
> One of the country's largest urban settlements of American Indians shares the streets with poor white youths, many from Appalachia. They call themselves the Gaylords or the Simon City Royals, and they war with rival gangs such as the Latin Kings. The tomb-gray lines of a government-funded high rise for low-income families tower over old hotels faced with ornately-sculptured arches and cornices which almost mock the misery of the elderly residents inside. And, along the lake shore, slick high rises "with a view" stand impervious to the poverty festering below them.

Guiding the parish raft through the Uptown maelstrom is Father Michael Rochford, a pastor who seems to enjoy the turbulence as he tries to keep the parish afloat:

> Our most serious problem here is trying to bridge the gaps and build one parish community. But the Burmese want to be with Burmese and the East Indians want to be with East Indians. They don't want an Irish priest telling them to play together. Sometimes I think it may not even be desirable for all nationalities to merge. I used to be a planner, but who could expect that one building which was all Filipino would go all black in three years? Or that we would have 134 Vietnamese families attending our church? My parents were Irish immigrants. I tell the Vietnamese when they come in that ultimately we are all immigrants. The church is the mainstay for newcomers. It's the one thing they have in common with their home country.
>
> It used to be that the Catholic church was the church of the working class. Now it is the country-club church of the middle class. We are still getting waves of immigrants, and the church is no longer at the shore to receive them. We have forgotten our origins, except in places like Uptown.

Father Rochford exaggerates. In 1950 Uptown had four Catholic elementary and secondary schools; Edgewater had six. Thirty years later in 1981, all ten schools were still around, the majority educating radically different—ethnically, racially and economically—students.

#9. Promote investment in older, multi-family buildings which, if not rehabilitated, are likely to be abandoned and eventually demolished, but which could be saved by converting them into condominiums.

If someone were to commission a poster which would vividly characterize the present condition of the Winthrop-Kenmore corridor, no symbol would be more appropriate than the empty, boarded-up apartment building. Not only are these residential tombstones dangerous (fires are endemic as squatters occupy them or as children play in them), but they create a neighborhood environment that strikes terror into the hearts of potential buyers or renters of surrounding properties.

What can be done with unprofitable, deteriorating, multi-story apartment buildings? Five alternatives, not all attractive, present themselves:

● *Turn* them into rooming houses, transient hotels or sheltered care facilities, packing them with the mentally ill, transients and derelicts for whom the government generally supplies the rent money. This has been the most popular solution since it usually requires that the owner need not invest money in any substantial renovation. Before long, these buildings simply wear out, become fire traps and are ravaged by fire; they then become vacant and are eventually demolished.

● *Sell* them at a bargain or donate them to a not-for-profit organization which will, in turn, rent to lower income families. To be successful, such a not-for-proft enterprise requires a large dose of idealism; a dedicated management willing to counsel and help tenants regarding jobs, alcoholism or language handicaps seven days a week; tenants and manager both ready to put their "sweat equity" into rehabilitating an apartment building; and bankers patient and sympathetic enough to take the risk and make a loan so that roofing, electrical and plumbing supplies can be purchased. Such combinations do exist in Uptown, but they are few in number. The most successful (relatively speaking) promoter of housing "fellowships" which save and remodel deteriorating apartment buildings to permit low income tenants to remain and become property managers is the Voice of the People. A not-for-profit group, the Voice seeks out multi-family buildings to rehabilitate, enlists the cooperation of the residents in doing some of the work and encourages tenant management. Despite the tender loving care showered upon tenant and property, the pace of success is discouragingly slow.

● *Tear* them down quickly before they self-destruct through theft, fire, and neglect.

● *Rehabilitate* them and rent the small apartments to the elderly poor who qualify for federal housing subsidies. The federal guarantees enable the owner to obtain a loan that will pay the costs of rehabilitation and thus ensure a steady income later from elderly residents who are likely to be good tenants.

● *Convert* them from rental apartments to ownership units via the condominium or cooperative route. To make such individual ownership of an apartment possible and desirable the developer has to undertake major rehabilitation to bring the building into full conformance with city codes and the buyer has to make an investment, the down payment. Under such circumstances, banks and savings and loan companies are more willing to invest their dollars. In recent years dozens of buildings in the corridor have been upgraded. Such behavior can be contagious. Owners next door or across the street, having seen what can be done and discovering that remodeling money can be found, soon decide to spruce up their own buildings.

In a community where obsolete apartment hotels and multi-family buildings predominate, they drag the surrounding area down with them. Mass media attention to condominium conversions, almost without exception, neglects this new avenue to neighborhood revitalization. The media publicize the spectacular conversion of newer, lakefront high-rise buildings to condominium ownership; the plight of elderly couples who earlier had sold their homes in order to spend their remaining days in a rental apartment close to Lake Michigan; and the hazards confronting purchasers of condominiums. Rarely do the media take note of the condominium tool for refurbishing larger properties with many apartments. It has enabled the owner to sell condominiums at terms attractive to families and individuals of modest means who seek the advantages of home ownership and who are taking a second look at the desirability of buying and moving into the corridor.

#10. Actively recruit the new "urban pioneers" ready to settle in the older sections of the city and to build new lives for themselves and their neighbors.

Children brought up in the suburbs, once they have gone away to college for four years, do not all return to their suburban arcadia. Some migrate to the countryside ringing the Chicago metropolitan area. Still others, especially singles and childless couples, venture into the city's older communities, like Uptown and Edgewater. In an age when more couples are postponing parenthood, urban homesteading seems, at least to them, less risky when children are not involved.

What are these inner city pioneers looking for? According to the population and demographics committee of the City Club of Chicago:

> Many young, white, middle and upper-middle class persons have decided to live on Chicago's near north and north sides... apparently a direct, conscious rejection of the suburban living option many older, and younger whites as well, have chosen.... The overwhelming reason...is the city's broad, multi-faceted "living efficiency"...inexpensive, relatively efficient mass transportation; easy access to employment, entertainment, and recreational activities; and multi-family housing that is readily available and relatively inexpensive, yet close to employment and entertainment...including the possibility of attending more events that are of a greater diversity in nature, meeting more different people, and basically being free to experience much more of what is novel in this day and age.

How many such urban adventurers actually are there? Nobody really knows as yet. They do exist, however, and their numbers seem to multiply from year to year. This has been the promising experience of Chicago's lakefront communities suffering from "people anemia" but anticipating a fresh supply of newcomers. The present residents, understandably euphoric and thinking wishfully, perhaps, imagine that hordes of urban frontiersmen are ready to move in if only someone would guide them to the Promised Land.

The City Club's report overlooked one influential colony of risk takers: young, married, college-educated couples expecting their first child. Their budgets can not withstand the high cost of suburban tri-level homes but can accommodate the lower prices of older houses in the inner city. Like the singles and childless couples attracted by the city's "living efficiency," the childbearing families are also willing to live there, provided that their children can get good schooling. Such educational expectations can be satisfied by public elementary education or, alternatively, by private schools. (In Edgewater and Uptown, parents have ample option among ten private Catholic schools, seven elementary and three secondary.)

To attract and retain such families, Edgewater primed the pump by promoting community self-confidence, marketing its amenities, and showing off the neighborhood. This was tried in a variety of ways. The Edgewater Community Council rented a booth at CITY HOUSE, a home improvement fair sponsored by the City of Chicago, to tell the Edgewater story. Catholic elementary schools in Edgewater sponsored open houses and printed individual brochures describing the distinctive educational program being given at each school. The principal of Senn public high school, with his staff and parents or students, talked to the graduating class at each of the public and Catholic grade schools in the community to encourage the students to enroll at his institution. Condominium owners on Sheridan Road have sponsored Sunday walks and tours along Winthrop and Kenmore Avenues to become acquainted firsthand with the two streets and the architecture of their buildings. Local realtors persuaded the North Side Real Estate Board to produce a "Community Guide" to depict the strengths of Edgewater and Uptown. In a flurry of merchandising, the Edgewater Community Council designed and sold jazzy "Viva Edgewater" T-shirts, marketed metal license plate attachments saying "Edgewater-U.S.A." and hung "Welcome to Edgewater" signs at key street intersections.

#11. Insist that city officials agree not to saturate the community's housing market with subsidized housing units but instead allocate to a community only its "fair share" of the city's total.

With regard to public housing, Chicago communities can be roughly divided into three kinds:

● Communities which already contain gigantic public housing projects that completely dominate the community's environment. Ordinarily, such communities are off limits for additional public housing units—because some federal judge has barred further construction.

● Communities which battle to keep public housing out. They do not want anything to upset their present racial and economic character. Because of their militancy and political prowess, such communities usually succeed in having the public housing built somewhere else in the city.

● Communities which are willing, freely or reluctantly, to let racial and economic integration take place. For religious, philosophical or political reasons they do not want their community to become exclusionary.

The first two groups represent the great majority of Chicago communities. During the 1970s, therefore, almost no public housing owned and operated by the Chicago Housing Authority or little of the subsidized housing allocated for privately-owned buildings found its way into these communities. Instead, federal, state and city agencies took the easy way out and concentrated their subsidized units in the third group of Chicago communities, far and away a minority. Lakefront communities generally fell into the third group. Their residential character, typified by the housing in the Winthrop-Kenmore corridor, was vulnerable to public policy and political ineptitude. Such communities often did not fully appreciate what was happening to their local housing market until years later when they discovered that thousands of federally subsidized units had been placed within their boundaries.

As a result, the northeastern corner of Chicago, covering Lakeview, Rogers Park, Edgewater and Uptown, and containing about nine percent of the city's population, in 1979 held thirty-three percent of the city's federal share of subsidized "Section 8" units available from the Chicago Housing Authority and a like proportion of "scattered site" public housing in walk-up buildings built since 1970. The large majority of these subsidized housing units could be found in the corridor. If various government agencies had their way, they would turn the corridor into one long "public housing project," only it would be privately owned and privately managed.

Only with limited success has Edgewater or Uptown been able to negotiate a "fair share" of such subsidized units for its community. Under pressure to satisfy federal guidelines calling for thousands of additional units of decent housing for low and moderate income families, the City acts as the broker. It carries enough legal authority to snub community demands. Furthermore, since Edgewater and Uptown already host large numbers of poor households, their presence weakens the bargaining power of those who plead for reducing the number of subsidized units. The former president of a neighborhood association, a renter, stated the dilemma with some feeling:

When we try to make the case for a "fair share" of such housing, there's always a coterie of do-gooders around to tag us racists, status seekers, or punishers of the poor, not only locally but downtown as well. Yet all we are trying to do is to prevent resegregation of the corridor. Right now the Winthrop-Kenmore corridor and its immediate area contain more "Section 8" subsidized units than does any other square mile in the United States. Even though we protest in a dignified and reasonable manner, we are labelled as bigots, oppressors of the poor, and social climbers who step upon the backs of the needy.

They tell me that it is bad public policy to build any more gigantic high-rise projects to shelter families eligible for public housing. I agree. They tell me that to concentrate dependent, single-parent families in a large project produces an unwholesome neighborhood environment. I agree. They tell me that it would be better if the poor were dispersed. I agree. But when I tell them it is bad public policy to swamp a community with thousands of subsidized housing units in privately-owned buildings and to overload a community with poverty and dependency, they shrug their shoulders.

Recently, enthusiasm has ebbed among public officials for subsidizing private developers to build high-rise apartments to be occupied predominantly by low and moderate income families. In Uptown, more than one such building constructed during the 1960s and 1970s has already deteriorated so badly that it has gone into bankruptcy. A janitor in one of these high-rises noted:

> Had I worked seven days a week, twelve hours a day, I couldn't keep up with the maintenance and refuse. I quit. So did the building manager. We couldn't work in a zoo. A building stacked with problem families doesn't work. You need a mix: solid citizens and striving couples to mingle with multi-problem families.

In Edgewater and Uptown, the issue of overstocking a community with subsidized housing remains unresolved in an era of conflicting priorities. Yet there is no doubt where most residents stand on the question. Brooks Miller, the director of the Hull House Center in Uptown, reflected the contemporary mood with regard to subsidized housing when he said:

> We are not against subsidized rental apartments. What we don't

want are any more large developers who tear down existing buildings and force families to move. We want no large buildings that are subsidized 100 percent. And we want no neighborhood to be highly impacted by subsidized housing.

#12. Capitalize on the strength and resources of an influential local institution whose own future is tied up with that of the community.

A sizable institution of higher learning can be a threat or an asset to a community. On the one hand, a university can be seen by its neighbors as an ornament, a source of pride and achievement, a happy convenience, a resource to be used when the need arises, a full-fledged participant in the local community. On the other hand, it can be regarded as an enemy that devours residential property, and its students as neighborhood nuisances. Often, the university can consider itself as a fortress fending off unfriendly neighbors seen as unsympathetic to an urban university's mission.

Loyola University's lake shore campus, located above the north end of Edgewater, is compact in size but large in numbers, enrolling more than 5,000 students. A board member of the Edgewater Community Council sized up the relationship between his community and the University:

> Most people see it as a community asset. Its institutional strengths have rarely collided with visible community objectives and have usually been used to support goals which the community itself has set. Even the University's recent purchase of multi-apartment buildings south of Devon Avenue for student housing has been viewed positively. Those buildings would have gone to the dogs otherwise.
>
> The biggest challenge is getting used to droves of students. Their kinetic energy amazes me; it bewilders others.

For years, in its community outreach, Loyola University had done the traditional things: supported financially the Rogers Park and Edgewater Community Councils and allowed its grounds to be used for fund-raising carnivals or its student lounges for community meetings. University faculty and staff were encouraged to serve on the committees and boards of the two community organizations.

By the late 1970s, the University's leadership recognized that such traditional activities were not enough. A premonition of what its position might be in another decade, if the blight creeping toward it down the corridor were not arrested, plus a genuine concern for the future of the community in which it had been housed for more than half a century, led the University to take unprecedented steps. The most dramatic and highly publicized of these was the inauguration of a "Walk-to-Work" program in 1977. Loyola's trustees established a $1,000,000 revolving loan fund to provide university employees with five-year, six percent loans of up to $8,000 to be used as a down payment on a home or condominium within walking distance of the campus. By 1981, three years later, fifty such loans had been made, leveraging nearly $3,000,000 in housing investment in the immediate vicinity, with almost half that amount going into the Edgewater community and the remainder into Rogers Park. The faculty and staff of Mundelein College, Loyola's next door neighbor, also became eligible for mortgage loans under the same program.

In addition, Loyola University funded its own "Community Program" through a storefront office off the campus to work with City officials, local churches, and community groups to improve neighborhood conditions. The Community Program was given a full-time director and a small staff. The new director, Megs Langdon, was not window dressing. She was an experienced community advocate and longtime member of the Chicago Plan Commission. The University's action electrified Edgewater residents who welcomed her professional help and expertise in their search for ways to revitalize the Winthrop-Kenmore corridor. The practical and symbolic importance of the University's program was pinpointed by Robert Wiedrich, a *Chicago Tribune* columnist:

> Ideally, a university should permeate a neighborhood with more than just its student body. It should also serve as a major force for good in the community, sharing the intellectual and cultural benefits of its programs and faculty by becoming deeply involved in community affairs. By its Walk-to-Work project, Loyola is doing just that — encouraging its staff to become active members of the neighborhood by acquiring a vested property interest.

* * *

When an inner city community is no longer split asunder by conflicting objectives, no longer confused about its priorities, and no longer frustrated by deferred decisions, it has a sporting chance to come alive once again. In such a planning climate both the urban pessimist and optimist are likely to remain around a little while longer to find out whether fresh approaches to community revitalization do indeed work. In the testing grounds along Winthrop and Kenmore Avenues, this unusual combination of older and newer urban strategies justifies guarded optimism. Edgewater is stemming the tide of dilapidation and lessening the fear of street crime. That is the message being delivered up and down the Edgewater section of the Winthrop-Kenmore corridor.

7

The Future of the Winthrop-Kenmore Corridor

During the 1980s the corridor does not suffer from the inattention of public and private decision-making. City planners have reappeared, this time directing their attention separately to the Uptown and Edgewater sections of the corridor. Significantly, the old "Uptown" designation used to cover both Uptown and Edgewater has been discarded in favor of a distinct planning strategy for each community. Breaking with precedent, the City officially has designated *two* Neighborhood Strategy Areas, one for Uptown and the other for Edgewater. The Winthrop-Kenmore corridor, except for its two northernmost blocks, has been incorporated into these Neighborhood Strategy Areas, making it eligible for Community Development funds coming from the Department of Housing and Urban Development.

Private initiatives in the Edgewater section of the corridor have become equally conspicuous. Hundreds of housing units are being rehabilitated, most to be rented as apartments; some to be sold as condominiums. Determinations remain. What is the future of the dozen apartment buildings which now stand vacant and boarded up? Will the housing court order them demolished? Or will they be bought and renovated? There is a further and highly sensitive question. Given the risks involved, will real estate investors rehabilitate occupied or vacant buildings only if the federal government subsidizes the housing units? As a sheltered care facility shuts down, what will be done with the building? Will it be returned to the private rental market? Or will it be reoccupied as another publicly-supported but privately-owned halfway house? Or will it operate unlicensed and unsupervised as an apartment "hotel" for former mental patients? And because of heavy wear and tear, will the building be eventually demolished? There is an ever-present fear of arson throughout the corridor. Will educational programs and new legislation, coupled with strict law enforcement, stamp out the epidemic of fires?

Some of the seedier blocks in the corridor are not to be found along Winthrop and Kenmore Avenues but on commercial streets which intersect them, running east and west. These are heavily used by pedestrians who travel them to reach the stations where they board the elevated train. Public officials have already started to give these run-down retailing strips prime attention. Will public improvements revive slipping businesses and attract new merchants? And will the City's cosmetic innovations (curb repairs, new sidewalks and better street lighting) restore confidence in a street's retailing future?

Several years ago the Chicago Transit Authority spent a small fortune completely re-doing Edgewater's busy elevated station at Bryn Mawr Avenue, while also installing an escalator and sprucing up the waiting platform. On this commercial street the remodelling was heralded as a major improvement, and indeed it was. What happened since? A disappointed shopper gave her view:

> The station's inside newsstand is no longer open, leaving a dirty, empty corner which looks depressing. The newsstand is now on the outside, blocking sidewalk traffic. Trash cans, broken beer bottles, old newspapers and rubbish litter the curb. It's a filthy sight. When they improved the station, they neglected to brighten up and improve the underpass on both sides of the street. The sidewalk area is poorly lighted and grimy, highly unappealing for pedestrian use.

Uptown is bothered by the same carelessness about minor but significant details. The newly-built Truman College was a community ornament. But in 1980 its large sign, visible to passengers riding the elevated, read "Harry S Truman Co lege." The "l" was missing for several months. Until its replacement, the college's sign advertised to the world that Uptown was an untidy place. An Uptown resident, however, noted:

> Why complain about Truman College? They fixed the sign within a few months. It would take anybody else years to get something that is a highly visible eyesore repaired.

For renters and owners, old-timers and newcomers, who live in the Winthrop-Kenmore corridor, the 1980s emerged as a fateful decade. The community's leaders are expected to set priorities to generate enough public and private momentum that will reverse downward trends. Most churches and synagogues flounder, looking around anxiously, ready to support others who might don the mantle of leadership. Scores of property owners hold back, deferring a decision on whether to renovate or sell. They await a sign that conditions have really begun to improve. Shrewdly, they suspect the platitudes of do-gooders and pollyannas, and take their cue, instead, from the actions of other property owners. They demand honest answers to questions which will reveal whether the corridor is indeed back on the road to recovery. The five questions most frequently asked are these:

1. Now that Edgewater has re-emerged as a viable and visible community, will it contend successfully with forces that suppress its newly-won identity?

Edgewater may have regained its identity in 1978, but keeping it was not easy. A sequence of events afterwards illustrated Edgewater's shaky possession of its own special character as outside forces, over which it had little or no control, once again went to work at erasing its image. These external influnces showed up in the most unexpected places, in institutions which most residents would regard as supporters of Edgewater.

In 1979, the publisher of Chicago's "neighborhood" telephone directories carved up Edgewater and provoked consternation and confusion among residents whenever they tried to find the telephone number of a neighbor or a local businessman. In trisecting Edgewater, the lakeside section (with half of the community's population) was sliced off and dropped into a *Lake Shore Directory* which listed most of the city's lakefront population north of Chicago's downtown area; the telephones of those who lived in the Uptown and Edgewater sections of the corridor were now listed in the *Lake Shore Directory*. The northwest section of Edgewater was slipped into the *Rogers Park Directory* which had fewer listings under "Edgewater" than did the *Lake Shore* book, and the rest of Edgewater was stuffed into a *Lincoln Square Directory*. Previously all of Edgewater's business and residential telephone numbers could be found buried in a single book, called, not surprisingly, the *Rogers Park-Uptown Directory*. Finally, the office of the Edgewater Community Council was listed in the *Lake Shore Directory* but not in the *Rogers Park Directory* which purported to be serving Edgewater.

Not long after receiving a free copy of her 1979 neighborhood directory, one Edgewater housewife exclaimed:

They sent me the wrong telephone book! It was the *Lincoln Square Directory*. Lincoln Square? Puzzled, I looked for my listing. Sure enough, my name and telephone were there. Till then I didn't even know that Lincoln Square existed. Was I surprised to find that I also lived there. Flicking through the pages, I quickly discovered that several stores I patronized were not listed. Nor were the names and telephone numbers of many neighbors.

Later I learned that the "lost" names and "missing" stores were listed in two other directories, the Rogers Park and Lake Shore ones. But again, I saw no sign of Edgewater, *my* community, in either of them. They had lost it. Now three neighborhood directories are piled on my shelf. When I go to look up a neighbor's number, I stop to figure out which book to use. I wonder. What made the telephone company slice up Edgewater and give the pieces to other communities? Should I use the city-wide telephone book instead? And chuck the neighborhood directories? They're nothing but a bother.

Over the years I tolerated the phone company's mislabelling my community as "Uptown." In retrospect, that was a big mistake. The company is now arrogant enough to stuff me into something they choose to call Lincoln Square. When I called to complain, the telephone supervisor replied with doubletalk, even claiming that I was the only person who had protested. But I knew better. Two of my neighbors had also called.

> Because Ma Bell is a corporate Goliath, why should we let her push us around? How do you appeal to a corporation that doesn't have a soul?

The omnibus Chicago telephone directory contained at least forty listings using the Edgewater name, including a hospital and three churches. Yet the promotional material used by the publisher, Reuben H. Donnelly Company, to sell advertising in the "yellow pages" of its neighborhood telephone directories, nowhere mentioned Edgewater on any of its nineteen maps.

Over the last two decades, the only community newspaper reporting Edgewater events has been the *Rogers Park-Edgewater News*, one of a successful chain of fifty-one neighborhood and suburban weeklies called the Lerner papers. In the 1970s the publisher began promoting a fifty-second edition, called *Skyline*, aimed at the high-rise residents living along the eight-mile stretch of Lake Michigan north of Chicago's center. For circulation, advertising and editorial reasons of his own, the publisher "detached" the lakeside portion of Edgewater and annexed it to *Skyline* which was distributed free to lakefront residents. Did the publisher eventually sense Edgewater's growing self-consciousness? In 1980 the publisher returned Edgewater's lakefront to the readership of the *Rogers Park-Edgewater News*.

The precarious economics involved in the publishing of the Lerner chain of weekly newspapers, each with an individualized community nameplate on page one, is not fully understood. But the eccentricities of such an editorial enterprise are not fully lost upon readers. One veteran subscriber to the *Rogers Park-Edgewater News* and a former journalist lamented:

> Edgewater doesn't really have a community newspaper. Most of what I see in my edition is advertising, entertainment and editorial boilerplate which appears in other Lerner editions. The amount of coverage actually given to Edgewater happenings is tiny. Replating the front page with the Edgewater logo and a smidgeon of local news, while the rest of the paper is basically the same, doesn't make it a local community newspaper or advocate. I happen to like the editorial policy of the Lerner chain; my wife likes the classified ads and the gossipy columnists. I wish I had the gumption and money to start a real community newspaper for Edgewater.

Despite such occasional detours, Edgewater's leadership continued confident that nobody would dare to run off with its hard-won prize: a community with its own name and identifiable boundaries.

2. Has Edgewater's section of the corridor become so saturated with low income families, with alcoholics and the mentally ill, with unemployed and unemployables, with drug addicts and prostitutes, that it will inevitably become like its Uptown counterpart?

What do you do when city, state and federal governments seem indifferent to the fate of a vulnerable pair of streets like Winthrop and Kenmore? When public agencies systematically exploit the corridor's obsolete and deteriorating housing so that their "community" programs, devised downtown, can be made to look good statistically? For nearly two decades government bureaucrats delivered, to Uptown's defenseless corridor, social traumas for which that community had not been prepared. Now Edgewater's segment of the corridor was being given the same treatment. One of Chicago's four large alcoholic detoxification centers is already located in the Edgewater section of the corridor; sixty-five percent of the men and women treated there each month are repeaters. It is no historical accident that in 1981 the Winthrop-Kenmore corridor found itself with a lion's share of the entire city's elderly poor, families on welfare, physically disabled, emotionally ill, drug users and alcoholics undergoing treatment in half-way houses, and former patients of the state's mental hospitals.

Only the city's large, high-rise, public housing projects, such as Robert Taylor and Cabrini-Green Homes, hold greater concentrations of poverty—more hard-core unemployed, more single-parent households and more families receiving public aid.

Taken together, Uptown and Edgewater house more than twenty percent of the entire city's licensed sheltered care facilities, including nursing homes and halfway houses. On the average, the Winthrop-Kenmore corridor is served by at least one social welfare agency per square block. Along Winthrop and Kenmore Avenues lie blocks where no less than fifty percent of the residents depend solely upon public assistance for their livelihood.

In the Uptown section of the corridor, most of the damage has already been done. During twenty years of "inundation," multi-family apartment buildings were turned into rooming houses. They were then so wilfully misused that eventually several thousand housing units, having become dilapidated and dangerous, had to be demolished. Acres of wasteland, once occupied by housing, deface the southern end of the Winthrop-Kenmore corridor. To revive Uptown's corridor in the 1980s, then, priority will have to be given to rebuilding it from the ground up, lot by lot and new brick by new brick.

Uptown's multi-ethnic character, its halfway houses, its political wars, its dilapidated stores, and its scattered graffiti make dramatic copy for lazy journalists. They can write feature articles for the magazine section of the Sunday newspaper or use their television cameras to package a three-minute filler on the 10 o'clock news. On the other hand, Uptown's own sturdy block clubs and neighborhood groups which push steadily for its revival rarely earn a headline, even though they represent the larger half of Uptown's present population and terrain. Lying to the east and west of the Uptown corridor and business center, these blocks and neighborhoods can play a decisive role in Uptown's future in the way that Edgewater's neighborhoods shaped their own community's future.

Not without heavy public debate and bitter conflict, a consensus is slowly being shaped: that the leverage needed to lift the entire Uptown community back onto its feet lies in the revitalization of its "downtown." How is this goal to be realized? Not by a nostalgic return to the glories of the 1920s but by developing a unique and urban blend of educational, residential, banking, business, and transportation amenities within a three block radius of Wilson and Broadway Avenues at the southern end of the Winthrop-Kenmore corridor. Here lies Uptown's center of gravity, this historic commercial and transportation hub around which Uptown's future revolves.

In acting upon its own agenda, Uptown may have to confront its own identity as a community. In the 1970s Edgewater finally succeeded in breaking away and shedding the image of "Uptown". Now Uptown has its own dilemma. In 1981 a resident of an Uptown neighborhood close to the lake revealed his own identity crisis:

> Why do you put me in Uptown? My neighbors and I live in Clarendon Park.

Clarendon Park describes his neighborhood. Uptown is the name of the community with which he now refuses to associate himself. He is not alone. In Uptown's western neighborhoods, further away from the lake, similar reactions occur. Residents again are prone to identify with their neighborhood, East Ravenswood, or South Andersonville, but reluctant, at times to make the community connection between themselves and Uptown. There are still other straws in the wind. To capitalize on the new presence of Truman College in the heart of Uptown, a recently-opened pharmacy and a new housing redevelopment corporation adopted the name "Truman Square". Others may follow suit. For Truman Square is "in", while Uptown is "out".

Sixty years ago Uptown was given its name by local businessmen who wanted to promote the fast-growing community emerging from the transportation center. In the 1980s, will the community retain its identity as Uptown? Or will it acquire a new image and a new name as part of its coming revival? Or will its neighborhoods, one by one, reweave the community once again as Uptown? A fascinating decade lies ahead.

In the Edgewater part of the corridor, irrevocable damage has not yet been done. The deteriorated housing can be rehabilitated. The decay is proceeding much more slowly than it did in Uptown decades earlier. Some large apartment buildings were abandoned, gutted by fires, and then had to be demolished; others still stand menacingly, vacant and boarded-up. But most of the buildings survive or thrive; their owners continue complaining that they have trouble locating reliable renters, while the tenants express dissatisfaction with the upkeep and services. Furthermore, the concentration of poverty in Edgewater has still a long way to go before reaching Uptown's level. The count of welfare recipients in Edgewater is only a fourth of the number who live in Uptown. Edgewater is still free of the industrial day labor agencies which spawned Uptown's skid row.

The task ahead in Edgewater then is to hold the line; to convince the downtown bureacracy that the corridor already holds more than its "fair share" of the chronically ill and welfare families; and to keep out the skid row which swamped Uptown and left it gasping for life.

But will such a strategy succeed in Edgewater? Most probably. To the corridor's east stands the impressive development of high-rise condominiums on Sheridan Road. They represent political and economic power. Then there is the influential network of Edgewater's westerly neighborhoods whose leaders have proved that they can help shape the community's future. Finally, the favorable outlook springs from the dynamics of the corridor's housing market.

Back in the 1960s high vacancy rates abounded in Uptown's multifamily buildings which were difficult to rent and uneconomic to renovate, hastening their deterioration. But the demand for the Edgewater corridor's supply of apartments, while erratic from year to year, never vanished the way it did in Uptown. Now in the 1980s, some of Edgewater's apartment hotels and high-rises, once regarded as superannuated, are being rehabilitated and restored to the general housing market at prices which renters or condominium buyers are quite willing to pay. In an era of frightening inflation the properties in the Winthrop-Kenmore corridor project the attractiveness shared by most older buildings in the central city. The high price of suburban real estate has steered the attention of thousands of home buyers and apartment seekers to the "housing bargains" to be found in the inner city. The Edgewater portion of the Winthrop-Kenmore corridor is slowly benefitting from this growing demand for the city's supply of older housing. If Edgewater succeeds in revitalizing its own segment of the corridor, that housing revival will make itself felt—back through the corridor across Foster Avenue into Uptown.

3. Will the present moratorium which bans any further licensing of halfway houses in the corridor remain effective?

Now almost a decade old, the moratorium has been far more than an aspirin providing temporary relief to the community. A local resident notes the difference:

> Some halfway houses have closed. They have not been replaced. We won't deny refugees from state mental health institutions

asylum in the corridor if they want to come here. But the large influx has declined, mainly because there no longer are that many mentally ill patients left in the state hospitals. The deluge is over.

The reprieve did accomplish this objective: giving the Winthrop-Kenmore corridor time to adjust, the communities a chance to plan. However, the communities' strategy of self-defense is being sapped by the unending multiplication of federally subsidized housing units in the corridor. Each year for more than a decade, the number of people living in subsidized housing in Uptown and Edgewater has skyrocketed, rising more rapidly here than in other communities of Chicago. The question for the 1980s is: How many subsidized housing units can a community absorb without itself being swallowed up by extreme poverty? A mother explains her worry:

> Many senior citizens will find a home here. That isn't bad. I don't object to poor people. I do object to prostitutes, drug peddlers and petty thieves. There are families on public aid who are fine neighbors. Their children go to the same school that my younsters attend.
>
> But when our pre-teens can identify the pimps and pushers on Bryn Mawr Avenue, their education may be a bit too liberal. I'd just as soon not encourage such educational opportunities for my family.
>
> Who are the people who bother me? They're con artists who cheat the government at our expense. Except for the public aid check each month, they deal strictly in cash. That's why they can easily qualify for a housing subsidy, and with it they can afford to live in new apartments which rent at $500 a month or more. What do you do about someone whose total income, legal and illegal, is far higher than yours? Who pays no income taxes? They're not the kind of neighbors to set my children a good example.

What is being achieved through the moratorium is at the same time being undermined by a tide of 6,000 units of subsidized housing in and around the Winthrop-Kenmore corridor.

4. When leprous-like housing shows up side by side with handsomely modernized properties, which trend, for better or worse, is likely to prevail throughout the corridor?

Winthrop and Kenmore Avenues in Edgewater are streets specked with highly visible, disconcerting contrasts. On one corner of Kenmore Avenue, for example, a prestigious developer finished the remodeling of a solidly built, handsome, seven-story high-rise late in 1979 and in 1980 began selling the thirty-eight units as condominiums priced from $29,000 to $65,000. Several months later, on Winthrop Avenue less than a block away, fires gutted two large, multi-family apartment buildings.

In the first fire, six people died. A bomb and arson investigator for the police department explained the possible cause:

> There were lots of prostitutes in the building, and a lot of people with backgrounds in prostitution. There was a lot of drug abuse in there. It could be any one of these.

Five weeks later, in a second fire across the street, four more persons died. Subsequently, a former mental patient was indicted for arson and murder; he was a man who had been under treatment in various state institutions for eighteen years prior to his release. A year later, a third disastrous fire swept through a transient hotel, one block north of the condominium development; nineteen persons died in the fire.

The front-page headlines about the fires were devastating in still another way. A prospective purchaser, then renting in a lakefront high-rise, said:

> We were set to buy a small building in the same block, around the corner from that sparkling building which had gone condo. After the two arsons, nobody could persuade us to buy. We wouldn't take the property even as a gift.

Uncertainty about the future of the corridor is not easy to resolve. Behind the questioning stands an assumption that Uptown's past sets the pattern for future change in Edgewater. That premise stresses the similarities between the two communities, their densely-built housing, their common core of mass transit, or their abundance of sheltered care facilities and boarding houses. Such a perspective, however, ignores the fundamental differences. Any promising forecast about Edgewater has to rely on a better understanding of its uniqueness, whether present or past. For the Edgewater optimist, these differences can be decisive:

● For several decades Uptown served as a major port of entry for out-of-town arrivals, unlike Edgewater which usually received such newcomers only after they had settled in Uptown and then began moving up the corridor. The one exception was the Cubans, who found their way to Edgewater first.

● Several thousand housing units were demolished in Uptown; only several hundred, at most, in Edgewater thus far. Furthermore, several thousand new apartments were built along Sheridan Road in Edgewater during the same decades. Who would have dreamed ten years ago that these high-rise condominiums would turn into vertical neighborhoods, their condo owners concerned with the future of their community—Edgewater?

The demographic changes that took place in Edgewater and Uptown between 1950 and 1980 are indicated in the two tables below.

EDGEWATER AND UPTOWN: POPULATION, 1950-1980, AND COMPARISON WITH CHICAGO POPULATION

Year	Chicago	Edgewater	Uptown
1950	3,620,962	54,606 (1.5%)[1]	84,426 (2.3%)
1960	3,550,404	51,579 (1.5%)	76,103 (2.1%)
1970	3,369,359	61,598 (1.8%)	74,838 (2.2%)
1980[2]	3,005,061	58,561 (1.9%)	64,414 (2.1%)

1. Figures in parentheses indicate percentage of Chicago population.

2. Between 1970 and 1980, Edgewater's population dropped by 4.9 per cent, Uptown's by 13.9 per cent, while the city's population as whole decreased by 10.8 per cent.

While the overall Chicago population decreased by seventeen percent during these three decades, Edgewater's rose by seven percent and Uptown's declined by twenty-four percent. Significant racial turnover began occurring in Uptown during the 1960s and continued throughout the 1970s. In Edgewater the racial shift became conspicuous in the 1970s. In both communities it was the

Winthrop-Kenmore corridor which first received most of the incoming blacks and other non-whites.

EDGEWATER AND UPTOWN: BLACK POPULATION, 1950-1980, AND PERCENTAGE OF EACH COMMUNITY'S POPULATION

Year	Edgewater		Uptown	
	Blacks	% of Pop.	Blacks	% of Pop.
1950	91	0.2%	436	0.5%
1960	53	0.1%	370	0.5%
1970	373	0.6%	3,045	4.1%
1980	6,514	11.1%	9,703	15.1%

During the same decades the number of housing units in Chicago city-wide rose about six percent. Uptown's remained about the same, but the number of housing units in Edgewater increased dramatically—by over fifty percent. The surge in Edgewater's housing units reflected the new high-rises built on Sheridan Road and the replacement of older housing stock along Winthrop and Kenmore Avenues by multi-family apartment buildings of much higher density.

● The bulk of the social welfare agencies, public and private, serving residents of the corridor can be found in Uptown. And they are not moving into Edgewater.

● A generation or so ago, when Uptown's supply of apartment buildings and hotels began filling up with a transient population, their landlords did not have condominium conversion as a viable option. Nowadays, in Edgewater, many multi-family apartment buildings, like those that were destroyed in Uptown, undergo renovation and then are returned to the conventional housing market as condominiums. Today, the Edgewater section of the corridor has proportionately more property owners than Uptown ever did.

● Except for the new and unexpected influx of subsidized housing during the 1970s, the mass migration into the corridor of former mental patients, alcoholics, drifters, and others who need and deserve kindly attention has slowed down. In the 1980s then, unless there is a shift in public policy, Edgewater will not have to contend with the surge in handicapped persons who engulfed Uptown in previous decades.

● Community efforts to revive Uptown in the 1960s were largely unsuccessful. They were led, for the most part, by businessmen who lived elsewhere. Their roots were not in Uptown. In contrast Edgewater's leaders, in the main, have historically been Edgewater homeowners or renters and church leaders. (For Uptown, it is a sign of hope in the 1980s that local residents now predominate among the community's outspoken leadership.)

● Furthermore, Uptown's community leadership is badly divided, the heritage of decades of frustration about the community's decline. Its many community organizations serve diverse and often warring constituencies, a spectrum from the radical left to the stubborn right. Major political battles have been resolved on election day by narrow margins, leaving future directions in doubt. Compared to Uptown, community leadership in Edgewater is far more united, generally agreeing on its priorities. After a good deal of discussion in 1979, the Edgewater Community Council pledged to "give first priority to...upgrading conditions along Winthrop and Kenmore." Robert Remer, president of the Edgewater Community Council in 1980 and 1981 and a resident of the Winthrop-Kenmore corridor, explained why he assiduously sought to keep Edgewater together:

> My aim was to avoid the polarization that divided Uptown. To deal with our problems we needed a united Edgewater. We refused to go along with those extremists who wanted us to take sides as they declared war on each other. The good of Edgewater came first. The Edgewater Community Council avoided being drawn into guerrilla warfare which would have weakened the community.

The differences between Edgewater and Uptown provide a perspective for an answer to a pair of controversial questions: What is the price to be paid for revitalizing the corridor? Is it the transfer of multi-problem households, lonely singles, and broken families to adjoining communities which will then be forced to repeat the painful experience of Uptown and Edgewater? A twenty-year resident of the corridor had this reply:

Displacement? That's a red herring in the corridor. Don't overlook the high mobility of corridor tenants. Many landlords rent their apartments without a lease; rent is on a monthly basis. In May of each year nobody is surprised to discover that a sixteen-apartment building had a total turnover of tenants during the previous year. Parts of the corridor are in constant motion with people moving in and out.

Relatively few people have to move because an owner intends to upgrade the building. Since remodeling takes place infrequently, dramatic displacement, involving large numbers of households, seldom occurs. Whenever it does, the tenants can still find vacant apartments in the corridor — if they can pay the rent and meet the landlord's standards which, fortunately for some tenants, are not that strict. Since the pace of improvement in the corridor is slow and steady, the impact elsewhere, if any, will go unnoticed.

What is frequently overlooked, in the scolding arguments over displacement, is that the commitment to house the poor has already been made and institutionalized. Walter Coleman of the Heart of Uptown Coalition notes:

> There are enough federally subsidized housing units in the corridor to guarantee a poor population of large size.

Given present trends, large-scale demolition resulting in wholesale displacement is unlikely to occur in the corridor. The present objective is to renovate existing properties and not to build new multi-family high-rises that will require destruction of existing housing. Under such conditions, possible confrontations over relocation seldom develop into anything serious. The following is a case in point. When the largest rehabilitation project ever attempted in the corridor was announced in 1979, opposition did arise. Ten buildings (seven in Edgewater and three in Uptown) with 300 apartments were to be renovated. But united support from Edgewater's political and community leaders paved the way for the improvement project to proceed. The appointment of an "oversight committee" to monitor relocation practices defused the opposition, as did the fact that many of the original tenants were able to move back into the renovated apartments.

5. Can neighborhoods and communities define their boundaries

without making their turf so exclusive that certain people can't move in? Can they act defensively without becoming exclusionary?

In Edgewater's neighborhoods such questions mystify residents who regard them as irrelevant and stereotyped. A Lakewood-Balmoral homeowner retorted:

> You're missing the whole point. We erected no barriers of race, class or ethnicity. We have tried to embrace the needy, the troubled and the anguished. We are not Camelot. But that doesn't give anyone the right to prejudge our motives and our actions.
>
> Exclusiveness is not the real issue. Inclusiveness is. We're trying to turn attitudes around so that everyone is important and receives respect. The suburbs highlight the kids who are winners. In the inner city the losers get the attention. What we want is a happier balance between these two emphases.

In the age of the nuclear family, the new urban neighborhood makes up, in part, for the decline of the extended family. The neighborhood is the helping network tied to a place. As a network of mutual support, the self-conscious neighborhood reaches out to help, calling upon a social agency only in an emergency. Some of the resentment against the proliferation of social agencies in Uptown and Edgewater arises from a desire to protect the neighborhood from the "downtown social delivery system" which is seen as ignoring and weakening the social fabric of the neighborhood.

Welfare agencies specialize in what is out of the ordinary: alcoholism, drug addiction, mental illness, juvenile delinquency, battered wives, abused children, and so on. As experts in pathology, their staffs are seen as underestimating the importance of those ordinary skills and strengths of "coping and communication," which a neighborhood fosters and upon which urban families rely. That is why the "vertical neighborhoods" which resulted from the conversion of Sheridan Road's high-rise apartments into condominiums also became networks of mutual support and sustenance.

In Edgewater today, the new urban neighborhood resists being compared to the ethnic enclaves of the past. The new urban neighborhood is multi-ethnic, varied economically and interracially, a mix of young, old, and those in between. As the Lakewood-Balmoral homeowner said:

> We want to attract all kinds of people. The only ones we don't welcome are the destructive, criminal types, and we had a few. We've had two big drug raids, with stake-outs and the works.
>
> Our schools are an experience. The boy who got the biggest hand at the sports banquet was a Laotian who probably had never seen a basketball until he arrived here. Nobody seems to be an outsider. My seventh grader had a birthday party last month that was attended by Orientals, blacks, Latinos and whites. I didn't plan it that way. Neither did she. It just happened naturally. These youngsters are more urbane and urban than their parents.

In the 1990s these youngsters will become Edgewater's owners and renters, and some may wonder how anyone in the 1980s could have been worried about the future of the Winthrop-Kenmore corridor.